Blueberry Hill

Casseroles & One Dish Meals

Notes for the reader:

All spoon measurements are level.

Unless otherwise stated milk is assumed to be whole and eggs are
medium-size.

Times given are an approximate guide only. Preparation times differ
according to different techniques used by different people and the
cooking times may also vary from those given as a result of the type
of oven used.

Sufferers from nut allergies should be aware that some of the ready-
prepared ingredients used in the recipes in this book may contain nuts.
Always check the packaging before use.

Recipes using raw or very lightly cooked eggs should be avoided by
infants, the elderly, pregnant women, convalescents, and anyone with
a chronic condition.

Contents

Welcome to Blueberry Hill

Here at Blueberry Hill we understand that busy families need easy and simple solutions. No one has the time to spend hours over a hot stove, when the kids need to be picked up from school, there's a deadline to reach at work and you need to conjure up something from the leftovers in the fridge. The good news is that with our recipes you can still feed your family good, honest, wholesome and nutritious meals but you won't feel like you are tied to your kitchen!

Our books are designed to introduce (or re-introduce) you to healthy, economical, and delicious food. Many of the recipes are lovingly remembered classics, while others feature familiar ingredients prepared from a fresh perspective.

Blueberry Hill Books are produced by a consortium of top-notch cooks and food professionals who have created a collection of hundreds of delectable family-style recipes, from appetizers to desserts. Each and every dish has been carefully tested, assuring perfect results every time.

Whether you consider yourself a gourmet or a beginning cook we're sure that our books will soon become a well-used collection on your shelf. In *Casseroles and One-Dish Meals*, you'll find a diverse and delicious range of 130 recipes. We've put together our favorite dishes, from classics such as *Yankee Pot Roast* and *Firehouse Chili Con Carne* to more exotic recipes such as *Spicy Aromatic Chicken*.

So, what more is there to say than, here's to enjoying less time in the kitchen and more time with the family!

Happy Cooking and warmest wishes from all of us at

Blueberry Hill

Pantry Essentials

A well-stocked pantry helps to make life a little easier when trying to plan out what to cook. The ingredients listed below are the things you'll regularly find on our shopping list.

Dry Ingredients

Pasta Spaghetti and macaroni are good basic pastas but for a broader choice add lasagna (sheets), Cannelloni (tubes), fusilli (spirals), farfalle (bows), tagliatelle (ribbons) and conchiglie (shells).

Rice Every pantry should have a good long-grain rice supplemented with basmati rice, risotto rice and brown rice.

Noodles Most noodles are associated with Asian cooking. Make sure you have a selection of both egg noodles and rice noodles for use in soups and stir-fries.

Flour All-purpose flour is great for thickening casseroles, making sauces and coating food before cooking. Self-rising flour is used for baking while bread making generally requires specific bread flour due to higher gluten levels.

Sugar White and brown sugar cover all the basic needs, but some recipes will call for confectioner's sugar for making frosting and for decoration.

Nuts and Seeds Walnuts, almonds, pine nuts and cashews can be used to add extra crunch and texture to savory dishes and baked goods. Make sure to store them in airtight containers. Sesame seeds are useful for many Asian inspired dishes.

Oils & Vinegars

Extra Virgin Olive Oil Ideal for drizzling over salads Extra Virgin Olive Oil is produced from the first cold-pressing of the olives and is a premium olive oil with a peppery, fruity flavor.

Vegetable Oil Made of a blend of various oils this is best used for frying, as it is very greasy.

Peanut Oil Suitable for drizzling, dressings and mayonnaise as well as other forms of cooking, this is a very versatile oil.

Wine Vinegars Available in many different varieties, mainly red, white and sherry. They can be used for dressings, marinades, and sauces or poured over foods.

Balsamic Vinegar This delicious vinegar is thick, dark and slightly sweet. It is made from grape juice that is aged in barrels over a number of years.

Herbs & Spices

Nothing beats fresh herbs or spices but it's always good to have the following dried herbs and spices to hand.

Chili Powder This powdered mixture of spices includes dried chiles, cumin, coriander and cloves. Use it to flavor soups and stews.

Paprika This spice is made from ground sweet red pepper pods and its flavor can vary from mild, sweet and pungent to fiery hot. It is excellent in salad and as a garnish.

Bay Leaves Originally from the Mediterranean dried bay leaves add a good pungent flavor to soups, sauces and casseroles. They are usually discarded once the food has absorbed their flavor.

Chives Relatives of the onion family these herbs can be added to salads, soups, cream cheese and egg dishes.

Garlic A must for any kitchen fresh cloves of garlic store well or you can buy jars of garlic cloves or dried garlic for your dishes.

Thyme A very versatile herb that can be used with meat, poultry, egg and potato dishes and is also good in soups, sauces, roasts, casseroles and stews.

Five Spice Chinese five spice seasoning is a blend of cloves, cinnamon, fennel seeds, Sichuan peppercorns and Star Anise. It is very popular in stir-fries.

Ginger Dried ginger is particularly good with fruit, cookies and condiments.

Apple Pie Spice This blend of spices usually consists of cinnamon, nutmeg and cardamom. It has a warm, sweet flavor and is delicious in fruit desserts, bread, cakes cookies, pies and drinks.

Other Items

Bouillon Cubes Great for use in casseroles and soups if you do not have time to make or buy fresh stock.

Tomato Paste This is a condensed puree, which adds a more intense flavor in sauces and soups.

Canned Tomatoes Always useful for a variety of dishes, from sauces and soups to stews and casseroles.

Canned Beans Always have a few cans of beans on hand from Red kidney beans, to lentils and chickpeas. They don't require soaking and can be very useful to have in any pantry.

Canned Fish Many dishes can use canned or fresh fish. Tuna, crab and anchovies are all useful for salads or pasta dishes.

Pickled Foods Pickles, pickled onions and capers make perfect accompaniments and garnishes for meat and vegetable dishes.

Olives It's always useful to have a can or a bottle of olives. They are delicious in salads, pastas and on pizzas or to blend and make dips from.

Soy Sauce A popular Chinese sauce it is used within many Asian foods and adds a salty flavor. Soy comes in light and dark varieties use the light one with shellfish and the dark one with duck and meat.

Worcestershire Sauce This spicy sauce adds a fantastic fiery flavor to casseroles and soups.

1

Poultry

Chicken Stew with Dumplings

serves 4

One 4 pound chicken, cut into quarters

2 tablespoons vegetable oil

2 leeks, trimmed, thoroughly washed, and sliced

2 large carrots, chopped

1 small parsnip, chopped

2 small turnips or pumpkin chopped

2½ cups chicken broth

3 tablespoons Worcestershire sauce

2 fresh rosemary sprigs

Salt and freshly ground pepper, to taste

Dumplings

1¾ cups self-rising flour

½ cup lard or vegetable shortening

1 tablespoon chopped rosemary leaves

Salt and freshly ground pepper, to taste

Remove the skin from the chicken (if you prefer). Heat the oil in a large, ovenproof casserole dish or heavy-bottom pan and sauté the chicken until golden brown. Using a slotted spoon, remove the chicken from the pan. Drain off the excess fat.

Add the leeks, carrots, parsnips, and turnips/pumpkin to the casserole dish and cook for 5 minutes, until lightly colored. Return the chicken to the pan.

Add the broth, Worcestershire sauce, rosemary sprigs, and salt and pepper to taste, then bring to a boil. Reduce the heat, cover, and simmer gently for about 50 minutes, or until the juices run clear when the chicken is pierced with a skewer.

To make the dumplings: Combine the flour, lard, and chopped rosemary, with salt and pepper to taste, in a bowl. Stir in just enough water to bind the ingredients to a firm dough.

Form into 8 small balls and place on top of the chicken and vegetables. Cover and simmer for an additional 10–12 minutes, until the dumplings rise. Serve immediately.

Chinese Chicken on Crispy Noodles

serves 4

8 ounces skinless, boneless chicken breasts, shredded

1 egg white

5 teaspoons cornstarch

8 ounces thin egg noodles

1²/₃ cups vegetable oil

2½ cups chicken stock

2 tablespoons dry sherry

2 tablespoons oyster sauce

1 tablespoon light soy sauce

1 tablespoon hoisin sauce

1 bell pepper, seeded and very thinly sliced

2 tablespoons water

3 scallions, chopped

Mix together the chicken, egg white, and 2 teaspoons of the cornstarch in a bowl. Let stand for at least 30 minutes.

Blanch the noodles in boiling water for 2 minutes, then drain thoroughly.

Heat the vegetable oil in a preheated wok. Add the noodles, spreading them to cover the base of the wok. Cook over low heat for about 5 minutes, until the noodles are browned on the underside. Flip the noodles over and brown on the other side. Remove from the wok when crisp and browned, place on a serving plate, and keep warm. Drain the oil from the wok.

Add 1¼ cups of the stock to the wok. Remove from the heat and add the chicken, stirring well so that it does not stick. Return to the heat and cook for 2 minutes. Drain, discarding the stock.

Wipe the wok with paper towels and return to the heat. Add the sherry, sauces, bell pepper, and remaining stock and bring to a boil. Blend the remaining cornstarch with the water and stir it into the mixture.

Return the chicken to the wok and cook over low heat for 2 minutes. Place the chicken on top of the noodles and sprinkle with the scallions.

Garlic Chicken & Bean Casserole

serves 4

4 tablespoons sunflower oil

2 pounds chicken meat, coarsely chopped

3 cups white mushrooms, sliced

16 shallots, peeled and left whole

6 garlic cloves, finely chopped

1 tablespoon all-purpose flour

1 cup white wine

1 cup chicken broth

1 tablespoon mixed herbs

One 14.5-ounce can cannellini beans, drained and rinsed

Salt and freshly ground pepper, to taste

Baked winter (butternut or acorn) squash, to serve

Preheat the oven to 300°F.

Heat the sunflower oil in a Dutch oven or an ovenproof casserole dish and sauté the chicken until browned. Remove the chicken from the casserole with a slotted spoon and set aside.

Add the mushrooms, shallots, and garlic to the casserole and sauté for 4-5 minutes, or until the vegetables begin to soften.

Return the chicken to the casserole and sprinkle with the flour, then cook for another 2 minutes. Add the white wine and chicken broth, stir until boiling, then add the mixed herbs. Season with salt and pepper to taste. Add the beans to the casserole.

Cover and cook in the preheated oven for 2 hours. Remove from the oven and serve with baked winter squash.

Red Hot Chili Chicken

serves 4

1 tablespoon curry paste

2 fresh green chiles, chopped

5 dried red chiles

2 tablespoons tomato paste

2 garlic cloves, chopped

1 teaspoon chili powder

Pinch of sugar

Pinch of salt

2 tablespoons vegetable oil

½ teaspoon cumin seeds

1 onion, chopped

2 curry leaves

1 teaspoon ground cumin

1 teaspoon ground coriander

½ teaspoon ground turmeric

One 14.5-ounce can chopped tomatoes

⅔ cup chicken stock

4 6-ounce skinless, boneless chicken breasts

4 cups freshly cooked rice, to serve

Fresh mint sprigs, to garnish

To make the chili paste, place the curry paste, fresh and dried chiles, tomato paste, garlic, chili powder, sugar, and salt in a blender or food processor, and process to a smooth paste.

Heat the oil in a large, heavy-bottomed pan. Add the cumin seeds and cook over medium heat, stirring constantly, for 2 minutes, or until they begin to pop and release their aroma. Add the onion and curry leaves and cook, stirring, for 5 minutes.

Add the chili paste, cook for 2 minutes, then stir in the ground cumin, coriander, and turmeric and cook for an additional 2 minutes.

Add the tomatoes and their juices, and the stock. Bring to a boil, then reduce the heat and simmer for 5 minutes. Add the chicken cover, and simmer gently for 20 minutes, or until the chicken is cooked through and tender.

Serve immediately with the rice and garnished with fresh mint sprigs.

Chicken & Rice One Pot

serves 4

⅔ cup long-grain rice

1 tablespoon dry sherry

2 tablespoons light soy sauce

2 tablespoons dark soy sauce

2 teaspoons firmly packed brown sugar

1 teaspoon salt

1 teaspoon sesame oil

2 pounds skinless, boneless chicken meat, diced

4 cups chicken stock

½ cup sliced mushrooms

½ cup water chestnuts, halved

1 cup broccoli florets

1 yellow bell pepper, sliced

4 teaspoons grated fresh gingerroot

Whole chives, for garnish

Cook the rice in a pan of boiling water for 15 minutes. Drain well, rinse under cold water, and drain again thoroughly.

Mix together the sherry, soy sauces, sugar, salt, and sesame oil.

Stir the chicken into the soy mixture, turning to coat well. Let marinate for about 30 minutes.

Bring the stock to a boil in a pan or preheated wok. Add the chicken with the marinade, mushrooms, water chestnuts, broccoli, bell pepper, and ginger.

Stir in the rice, reduce the heat, cover, and cook for 25–30 minutes, until the chicken and vegetables are cooked through. Transfer to serving plates, garnish with the chives, and serve.

Garlic & Lime Chicken

serves 4

Four 6-ounce skinless, boneless chicken breasts

3 tablespoons garlic butter, softened

3 tablespoons chopped fresh cilantro

1 tablespoon vegetable oil

Finely grated zest and juice of 2 limes, plus extra zest, for garnish

4 tablespoons firmly packed brown sugar

Boiled rice and lemon wedges, for serving

Place each chicken breast between 2 sheets of plastic wrap and pound with a rolling pin until flattened to about ½-inch thick.

To make the garlic butter mix 3 tablespoons of softened butter with two cloves of finely chopped garlic.

Mix together the garlic butter and cilantro and spread over each flattened chicken breast. Roll up like a jelly roll and secure with a toothpick.

Heat the oil in a preheated wok or heavy bottom skillet.

Add the chicken rolls to the wok and cook, turning, for 15–20 minutes or until cooked through.

Remove the chicken from the wok and transfer to a board. Cut each chicken roll into slices.

Add the lime zest and juice and sugar to the wok and heat gently, stirring, until the sugar has dissolved. Raise the heat and allow to bubble for 2 minutes.

Arrange the chicken on warmed serving plates and spoon over the juices to serve.

Garnish with extra lime zest, if desired, and serve with the boiled rice and lemon wedges.

Louisiana Chicken

serves 4-6

5 tablespoons corn oil

4 chicken pieces

6 tablespoons all-purpose flour

1 onion, chopped

2 celery stalks, sliced

1 green bell pepper, seeded and chopped

2 garlic cloves, finely chopped

2 teaspoons chopped fresh thyme

2 fresh red chiles, seeded and finely chopped

One 14.5-ounce can chopped tomatoes

1¼ cups chicken stock

Salt and pepper

Chopped fresh thyme, to garnish

Heat the oil in a large, heavy-bottom saucepan or flameproof casserole. Add the chicken and cook over medium heat, stirring, for 5–10 minutes or until golden. Transfer the chicken to a plate with a slotted spoon.

Stir the flour into the oil and cook over very low heat, stirring constantly, for 15 minutes, or until light golden. Do not let it burn. Immediately add the onion, celery, and green bell pepper and cook, stirring constantly, for 2 minutes. Add the garlic, thyme, and chiles and cook, stirring, for 1 minute.

Stir in the tomatoes and their juices, then gradually stir in the stock. Return the chicken pieces to the pan, cover, and simmer for 45 minutes, or until the chicken is cooked through and tender.

Season to taste with salt and pepper, transfer to warmed serving plates, and serve immediately, garnished with a sprinkling of chopped thyme.

Orange Turkey with Rice

serves 4

1 tablespoon olive oil

1 medium onion, chopped

1 pound skinless turkey breast cutlets, cut into thin strips

1¼ cups unsweetened orange juice

1 bay leaf

3 cups small broccoli florets

1 large zucchini, diced

1 large orange

6 cups cooked brown rice

Salt and freshly ground pepper, to taste

9–10 pitted black olives, drained and quartered, to garnish

Shredded basil leaves, to garnish

Heat the oil in a large skillet and cook the onion and turkey, stirring, for 4–5 minutes, until lightly browned.

Pour in the orange juice and add the bay leaf and seasoning. Bring to a boil and simmer for 10 minutes.

Meanwhile, bring a large pan of water to a boil and cook the broccoli florets, covered, for 2 minutes. Add the diced zucchini, then bring back to a boil. Cover and cook for another 3 minutes. Drain and set aside.

Using a sharp knife, peel off the skin and white pith from the orange. Slice down the orange to make thin circular slices, then halve each slice.

Stir the broccoli, zucchini, rice, and orange slices into the turkey mixture. Gently mix together and season, then heat through for another 3–4 minutes, or until the mixture is piping hot.

Transfer the turkey rice to warm serving plates and garnish with black olives and shredded basil leaves.

One Pot Spicy Chicken & Noodles

serves 4

1 tablespoon vegetable oil

1 onion, sliced

1 garlic clove, crushed

1-inch piece of fresh gingerroot, peeled and grated

6 scallions, sliced diagonally

1 pound chicken breast fillet, skinned and cut into pieces

2 tablespoons mild curry paste

2 cups coconut milk

1¼ cups chicken stock

9 ounces egg noodles

2 teaspoon lime juice

Pinch of salt

Freshly ground black pepper

Heat the oil in a wok or large heavy-bottom skillet.

Add the onion, garlic, ginger, and scallions to the wok and stir-fry for 2 minutes until softened.

Add the chicken and curry paste and stir-fry for 4 minutes, or until the vegetables and chicken are golden brown. Stir in the coconut milk, stock, and salt and pepper to taste, and mix well.

Bring to a boil, add the noodles to the pan, cover, and simmer for about 6–8 minutes until the noodles are just tender, stirring occasionally.

Add the lime juice and adjust the seasoning and serve immediately.

Orange Chicken Casserole

serves 4

2 tablespoons vegetable oil

1 chicken, weighing about 3 pounds 5 ounces

2 large oranges

2 small onions, cut into quarters

3 small whole carrots or thin carrots, cut into 2-inch lengths

2/3 cup orange juice

2 tablespoons brandy

2 tablespoons sesame seeds

1 tablespoons cornstarch

Pinch of salt

Freshly ground black pepper

Preheat the oven to 350°F.

Heat the oil in a large flameproof casserole and fry the chicken, turning occasionally until evenly browned.

Cut one orange in half and place half inside the cavity of the chicken. Place the chicken in a large, deep casserole.

Arrange the onions and carrots around the chicken. Season with salt and pepper and pour over the orange juice.

Cut the remaining orange into thin wedges and tuck around the chicken, between the vegetables.

Cover and cook in a preheated oven for about 1½ hours, or until the chicken juices run clear when pierced and the vegetables are tender. Remove the lid and sprinkle with the brandy and sesame seeds. Return to the oven for 10 minutes.

To serve, lift the chicken onto a large platter and add the vegetables. Skim any excess fat from the juices. Blend the cornstarch with 1 tablespoon cold water, then stir into the juices and bring to a boil, stirring all the time. Adjust to taste, then serve the sauce with the chicken.

Coq Au Vin

serves 4

¼ cup (1 stick) butter

2 tablespoons olive oil

4 pounds chicken pieces

6 slices rindless smoked bacon, cut into strips

12 pearl onions, peeled

12 cremini mushrooms, halved

2 garlic cloves, finely chopped

2 tablespoons brandy

1 cup red wine

1¼ cups chicken stock

1 tablespoon dried mixed herbs

1 bay leaf

2 tablespoons all-purpose flour

Salt and pepper

Melt half the butter with the olive oil in a large, flameproof casserole. Add the chicken and cook over medium heat, stirring, for 8–10 minutes, or until golden brown. Add the bacon, onions, mushrooms, and garlic.

Pour in the brandy and set it alight with a match or taper. When the flames have died down, add the wine, stock, mixed herbs, bay leaf, and season to taste with salt and pepper.

Bring to a boil, reduce the heat, and simmer gently for 1 hour, or until the chicken pieces are cooked through and tender. Meanwhile, make a paste by mashing the remaining butter with the flour in a small bowl.

Remove and discard the bay leaf. Transfer the chicken to a large plate and keep warm. Stir the beurre manié into the casserole, a little at a time. Bring to a boil, return the chicken to the casserole, and serve immediately.

Duck & Vegetable Stew with Red Wine

serves 4

Four (5-6 ounce) duck portions (usually halves)

1–2 teaspoons olive oil, plus 1 tablespoon (optional)

1 red onion, cut into wedges

2–3 garlic cloves, chopped

1 large carrot, chopped

2 stalks celery, chopped

2 tablespoons all-purpose flour

1¼ cups red wine

2 tablespoons brandy (optional)

²/₃–¾ cup stock or water

Salt and freshly ground pepper, to taste

3-inch strip of orange rind

1 cup sugar snap peas

1 cup small white mushrooms

1 tablespoon chopped fresh parsley, to garnish

Remove and discard the fat from the duck. Lightly rinse the duck pieces and pat dry with paper towels.

Heat a large, deep skillet for 1 minute until warm but not piping hot. Put the duck halves in the skillet and heat gently until the fat starts to run. Increase the heat a little, then cook, turning over halfway through, for 5 minutes, or until browned on both sides and sealed. Using a slotted spoon, transfer the duck halves to a flameproof casserole dish.

Add 1 tablespoon of the oil (if there is little duck fat remaining in the skillet), and cook the onion, garlic, carrot, and celery, stirring frequently, for 5 minutes, or until the vegetables have softened. Sprinkle in the flour and cook, stirring constantly, for 2 minutes, then remove the skillet from the heat.

Gradually stir in the wine, brandy (if using), and stock, then return the pan to the heat and bring to a boil, stirring. Season to taste with salt and pepper, then add the orange rind. Pour the sauce over the duck portions in the casserole, then cover and simmer, stirring occasionally, for 1–1¼ hours.

Cook the sugar snap peas in a pan of boiling water for 3 minutes, then drain and add to the stew. Meanwhile, heat 1–2 teaspoons of the olive oil in a small pan and cook the mushrooms, stirring frequently, for 3 minutes, or until the mushrooms begin to soften. Add to the stew. Cook the stew for an additional 5 minutes, or until the duck is tender. Serve garnished with the chopped parsley.

Sage Chicken with Rice

serves 4

1 large onion, chopped

1 garlic clove, crushed

2 stalks celery, sliced

2 carrots, diced

2 sprigs fresh sage

1¼ cups chicken stock

12 ounces boneless, skinless chicken breasts

10 ounces mixed brown and wild rice

One 14.5-ounce can chopped tomatoes

Dash of Tabasco sauce

2 medium zucchini, trimmed and thinly sliced

4 ounces lean ham, diced

Pinch of salt

Freshly ground black pepper

Fresh sage, for garnish

Place the pieces of onion, garlic, celery, carrots, and sprigs of sage in a large pan and pour in the stock.

Bring to a boil, cover the pan, and simmer for 5 minutes.

Cut the chicken into 1-inch cubes and stir into the pan with the vegetables. Cover the pan and continue to cook for an additional 5 minutes.

Stir in the rice and the tomatoes.

Add a dash of Tabasco sauce to taste and season well. Bring to a boil, cover, and simmer for 25 minutes.

Stir in the zucchini and the ham and continue to cook, uncovered, for an additional 10 minutes, stirring occasionally, until the rice is just tender.

Remove and discard the sprigs of sage. Serve immediately.

Chicken & Butternut Squash Casserole

serves 4

2 tablespoons olive oil

Four 3½-ounce skinless, boneless chicken thighs, cut into bite-size pieces

1 large onion, sliced

2 leeks, trimmed, thoroughly washed, and chopped

2 garlic cloves, chopped

1 butternut squash, peeled, seeded, and cut into cubes

2 carrots, diced

One 14.5-ounce can chopped tomatoes with herbs

One 14.5-ounce can mixed beans, drained and rinsed

½ cup vegetable or chicken broth, plus extra if needed

Salt and freshly ground pepper, to taste

Preheat the oven to 325°F.

Heat 1 tablespoon of the oil in a large, ovenproof casserole over high heat, then add the chicken and cook, turning frequently, for 2–3 minutes, or until browned all over. Reduce the heat to medium, then remove the chicken with a slotted spoon and set aside.

Add 1 tablespoon of the oil to the casserole dish, then add the onion and leeks and cook, stirring occasionally, for 10 minutes, or until softened. Add the garlic, squash, and carrots, and cook, stirring, for 2 minutes. Add the tomatoes, beans, and stock, then stir well and bring to a simmer.

Cover, then transfer to the preheated oven and cook for 1–1¼ hours, stirring once or twice. If the casserole looks too dry, add a little extra stock. Season to taste with salt and pepper. Serve immediately.

Chicken & Fall Vegetable Casserole

serves 4

3 tablespoons olive oil

2 leeks, sliced

2 garlic cloves, sliced

2 large chicken breasts, 6 ounces cut into bite-size pieces

2 sweet potatoes, peeled and cut into chunks

2 parsnips, scrubbed and sliced

1 red bell pepper, seeded and cut into strips

1 yellow bell pepper, seeded and cut into strips

2 cups mixed mushrooms

3 cups coarsely chopped tomatoes

4 cups cooked white long-grain rice

1 small bunch fresh parsley, chopped

1 cup cheddar cheese, grated

Pinch of salt and freshly ground black pepper

Preheat the oven to 350°F.

Heat the oil in a large skillet over medium heat, then add the leeks and garlic and cook, stirring frequently, for 3–4 minutes, or until softened. Add the chicken and cook, stirring frequently, for 5 minutes.

Add the sweet potatoes and parsnips and cook, stirring frequently, for 5 minutes, or until golden and beginning to soften. Add the bell peppers and mushrooms and cook, stirring frequently, for 5 minutes.

Stir in the tomatoes, rice, and parsley and season to taste with salt and pepper.

Spoon the mixture into an ovenproof dish. Scatter over the cheddar cheese and bake in the preheated oven for 20–25 minutes. Serve immediately.

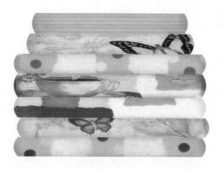

Chicken Peperonata

serves 4

8 chicken thighs

2 tablespoons whole-wheat flour

2 tablespoons olive oil

1 small onion, thinly sliced

1 garlic clove, crushed

1 large red bell pepper, seeded and thinly sliced

1 large yellow bell pepper, seeded and thinly sliced

1 large green bell pepper, seeded and thinly sliced

One 14.5-ounce can chopped tomatoes

1 tablespoon chopped fresh oregano

Pinch of salt

Freshly ground black pepper

Crusty whole wheat bread, for serving

Remove the skin from the chicken thighs and toss the meat in the flour.

Heat the oil in a wide skillet and fry the chicken over medium heat until sealed and lightly browned, then remove from the skillet.

Add the onion to the skillet, reduce the heat, and cook, stirring occasionally, for about 5 minutes until softened, but not browned. Add the garlic, bell pepper slices, tomatoes, and oregano, then bring to a boil, stirring continuously.

Arrange the chicken on top of the vegetables, season with salt and pepper to taste, then cover the pan tightly, and simmer for 20–25 minutes or until the chicken is completely cooked and tender.

Taste and adjust the seasoning, if necessary. Transfer the chicken to a plate. Spoon the vegetables onto a warmed serving platter and top with the chicken. Serve immediately with the bread.

Chicken & Apple Casserole

serves 4

4 6-ounce skinless chicken breasts

1 tablespoon olive oil

1 onion, chopped

2 celery ribs, coarsely chopped

1½ tablespoons all-purpose flour

1¼ cups clear apple juice

⅔ cup chicken stock

1 baking apple, peeled, cored, and cut into quarters

2 bay leaves

1–2 teaspoons honey

1 yellow bell pepper, seeded and cut into chunks

Salt and freshly ground pepper

1 tablespoon butter

2 medium apples, peeled, cored, and sliced

2 tablespoons firmly packed light brown sugar

1 tablespoon chopped fresh mint, to garnish

Preheat the oven to 375°F. Lightly rinse the chicken and pat dry with paper towels.

Heat the oil in a deep skillet and cook the chicken over medium–high heat, turning frequently, for 10 minutes, or until golden and sealed. Using a slotted spoon, transfer the chicken to an ovenproof casserole.

Add the onion and celery to the skillet and cook over medium heat, stirring frequently, for 5 minutes, or until softened. Sprinkle in the flour and cook, stirring constantly, for 2 minutes, then remove from the heat.

Gradually stir in the apple juice and stock, then return to the heat and bring to a boil, stirring constantly. Add the baking apple, bay leaves, and honey, and season to taste with salt and pepper.

Pour the sauce over the chicken in the casserole, then cover and cook in the preheated oven for 25 minutes. Add the bell pepper and cook for an additional 10–15 minutes, or until the chicken is tender and the juices run clear when a skewer is inserted into the thickest part of the meat.

To prepare the apples: Preheat the broiler to high. Melt the butter in a pan over low heat. Line the broiler pan with aluminum foil. Brush the eating apple slices with half the butter, then sprinkle with a little brown sugar and cook under the broiler for 2–3 minutes, or until the sugar has caramelized. Turn the slices over. Brush with the remaining butter and sprinkle with the remaining sugar, and cook for an additional 2 minutes. Serve the stew garnished with the apple slices and mint.

Chicken in White Wine

serves 4

4 tablespoons (½ stick) butter

2 tablespoons olive oil

2 thick, rindless, lean bacon strips, chopped

8 pearl onions, peeled

1 garlic clove, finely chopped

One 4-pound chicken, cut into 8 pieces

1¾ cups dry white wine

1¼ cups chicken broth

1 tablespoon mixed dry herbs

1 bay leaf

1 cup button mushrooms

2½ tablespoons all-purpose flour

Salt and freshly ground pepper, to taste

Fresh herb sprigs, to garnish

Preheat the oven to 325°F.

Melt 2 tablespoons butter with the oil in an ovenproof casserole dish. Add the bacon and cook over medium heat, stirring, for 5–10 minutes, or until golden brown.

Transfer the bacon to a large plate. Add the onions and garlic to the casserole dish and cook over low heat, stirring occasionally, for 10 minutes, or until golden. Transfer to the plate. Add the chicken and cook over medium heat, stirring constantly, for 8–10 minutes, or until golden. Transfer to the plate.

Drain off any excess fat from the casserole. Stir in the wine and broth and bring to a boil, scraping any sediment off the bottom. Add the bay leaf and herbs and season to taste. Return the bacon, onions, and chicken to the casserole. Cover and cook in the preheated oven for 1 hour. Add the mushrooms, re-cover, and cook for 15 minutes. Meanwhile, make a beurre manié by mashing 2 tablespoons butter with the flour in a small bowl.

Remove the casserole from the oven and set over medium heat. Remove and discard the bay leaf. Whisk in the beurre manié, a little at a time. Bring to a boil, stirring constantly, then serve, garnished with fresh herb sprigs.

Italian Style Roast Chicken

serves 6

6 pounds chicken

Sprigs of fresh rosemary

1 cup grated feta cheese

2 tablespoons sun-dried tomato paste

4 tablespoons butter, softened

1 bulb garlic

2 pound 4 ounces new potatoes, halved if large

1 each red, green, and yellow bell pepper, seeded and cut into chunks

3 zucchini, thinly sliced

2 tablespoons olive oil

2 tablespoons all-purpose flour

2½ cups chicken stock

Salt and pepper

Preheat the oven to 375°F.

Rinse the chicken inside and out with cold water and drain well. Carefully cut between the skin and the top of the breast meat using a small pointed knife. Slide a finger into the slit and carefully enlarge it to form a pocket. Continue until the skin is completely lifted away from both breasts and the top of the legs.

Chop the leaves from 3 rosemary stems. Mix with the feta cheese, sun-dried tomato paste, butter, and pepper to taste, then spoon under the skin. Put the chicken in a large roasting pan, cover with foil, and cook for 20 minutes per 1 pound plus 20 minutes.

Break the garlic bulb into cloves but do not peel. Add the vegetables and garlic to the chicken after 40 minutes, drizzle with oil, tuck in a few stems of rosemary, and season with salt and pepper. Cook for the remaining calculated time, removing the foil for the last 40 minutes to brown the chicken.

Transfer the chicken to a serving platter. Place some of the vegetables around the chicken and transfer the remainder to a warmed serving dish. Spoon the fat (it will be floating on top) out of the roasting pan and stir the flour into the remaining cooking juices. Place the roasting pan on top of the stove and cook over medium heat for 2 minutes, then gradually stir in the stock. Bring to a boil, stirring, until thickened. Strain into a sauce boat and serve with the chicken.

Spanish Lemon Chicken

serves 4

1 tablespoon all-purpose flour

4 6-ounce chicken portions

2 tablespoons olive oil

2 garlic cloves, crushed

1 large Spanish onion, thinly sliced

3 cups chicken stock

½ teaspoon saffron threads

2 yellow bell peppers, seeded and cut into chunks

2 preserved lemons, cut into quarters

10 ounces brown basmati rice

Pinch white pepper

12 pimiento-stuffed green olives

Preheat the oven to 350°F.

Put the flour into a large freezer bag. Add the chicken, close the top of the bag, and shake to coat with flour.

Heat the oil in a large skillet over low heat, add the garlic, and cook for 1 minute, stirring constantly.

Add the chicken to the skillet and cook over medium heat, turning frequently, for 5 minutes, or until the skin is lightly browned, then remove to a plate. Add the onion to the skillet and cook, stirring occasionally, for 10 minutes until softened.

Meanwhile, put the stock and saffron into a pan over low heat and heat through.

Transfer the chicken and onion to a large casserole dish, add the bell peppers, lemons, and rice, then pour over the stock. Mix well and season with pepper to taste.

Cover and cook in the preheated oven for 50 minutes, or until the chicken is cooked through and tender. Reduce the oven temperature to 325F. Add the olives to the casserole and cook for an additional 10 minutes.

Sunshine Chicken

serves 4

1 pound skinless, boneless chicken breasts

1½ tablespoons all-purpose flour

Salt and freshly ground pepper, to taste

1 tablespoon olive oil

1 onion, cut into wedges

2 celery ribs, sliced

²/₃ cup orange juice

1¼ cups chicken broth

1 tablespoon light soy sauce

1–2 teaspoons clear honey

1 tablespoon grated orange rind

1 orange bell pepper, seeded and chopped

1–2 zucchini, sliced into semicircles

2 small corn cobs, halved, or ½ cup corn kernels

1 orange, peeled and segmented

1 tablespoon chopped fresh parsley, to garnish

Lightly rinse the chicken and pat dry with paper towels. Cut into bite-size pieces. Season the flour well with salt and pepper. Toss the chicken in the seasoned flour until well coated and reserve any remaining seasoned flour.

Heat the oil in a large, heavy-bottom skillet and cook the chicken over high heat, stirring frequently, for 5 minutes, or until golden on all sides and sealed. Using a slotted spoon, transfer to a plate.

Add the onion and celery to the skillet and cook over medium heat, stirring frequently, for 5 minutes, or until softened. Sprinkle in the reserved seasoned flour and cook, stirring constantly, for 2 minutes, then remove from the heat. Gradually stir in the orange juice, broth, soy sauce, and honey, followed by the orange rind, then return to the heat and bring to a boil, stirring.

Return the chicken to the skillet. Reduce the heat, then cover and simmer, stirring occasionally, for 15 minutes. Add the orange bell pepper, zucchini, and corn and simmer for an additional 10 minutes, or until the chicken and vegetables are tender. Add the orange segments, then stir well and heat through for 1 minute. Serve garnished with the parsley.

Chicken & Chorizo Casserole

serves 4

3 tablespoons olive oil

One 5-pound chicken, cut into 8 pieces and dusted with flour

8 ounces fresh chorizo sausages, thickly sliced

3 tablespoons chopped fresh sage

1 onion, chopped

6 garlic cloves, peeled and sliced

2 celery stalks, sliced

1 small pumpkin or butternut squash, peeled and coarsely chopped

1 cup dry sherry

2½ cups chicken broth

One 14.5-ounce can chopped tomatoes

2 bay leaves

Salt and freshly ground pepper, to taste

3-4 tablespoons chopped fresh Italian parsley

Preheat the oven to 350°F.

Heat the oil in a Dutch oven or flameproof casserole and fry the chicken with the chorizo and sage leaves until golden brown. Remove the meat with a slotted spoon and reserve. (You may need to do this in batches.)

Add the onion, garlic, celery, and pumpkin to the casserole, and cook until the vegetables begin to brown slightly. Add the sherry, chicken broth, tomatoes, and bay leaves, and season with salt and pepper to taste.

Return the reserved chicken, chorizo, and sage to the casserole, cover, and cook in the oven for 1 hour. Remove the casserole from the oven, uncover, stir in the chopped parsley and serve.

Chicken Jambalaya

1 pound skinless, boneless chicken breast, diced

1 red onion, diced

1 garlic clove, crushed

2½ cups chicken stock

One 14.5-ounce can chopped tomatoes in tomato juice

1½ cups brown rice

1–2 teaspoons hot chili powder

½ teaspoon paprika

1 teaspoon dried oregano

1 red bell pepper, seeded and diced

1 yellow bell pepper, seeded and diced

¾ cup frozen corn

1 cup frozen peas

Put the chicken, onion, garlic, stock, tomatoes, and rice into a large heavy-bottom pan. Add the chili powder, paprika, and oregano and stir well. Bring to a boil, then reduce the heat, cover, and let simmer for 25 minutes.

Add the bell peppers, corn, and peas to the rice mixture and return to a boil.

Reduce the heat, cover, and let simmer for an additional 10 minutes, or until the rice is just tender (brown rice retains a nutty texture when cooked) and most of the stock has been absorbed but is not completely dry.

Serve immediately.

Chicken with Green Olives

serves 4

3 tablespoons olive oil

2 tablespoons butter

4 6-ounce chicken breasts

1 large onion, finely chopped

2 garlic cloves, crushed

2 red, yellow, or green bell peppers, cored, seeded and cut into large pieces

¾ cup small mushrooms, sliced

6 tomatoes, peeled and halved

⅔ cup dry white wine

1½ cups pitted green olives

4–6 tablespoons heavy cream

12 ounces dried pasta shapes

Pinch of salt

Freshly ground black pepper

Preheat the oven to 350°F.

Heat 2 tablespoons of the oil and the butter in a skillet. Add the chicken breasts and fry until golden brown all over. Remove the chicken from the skillet.

Add the onion and garlic to the skillet and fry over medium heat until beginning to soften. Add the bell peppers and mushrooms and cook for 2–3 minutes.

Add the tomatoes and season with salt and pepper to taste. Transfer the vegetables to a casserole and arrange the chicken on top.

Add the wine to the skillet and bring to a boil. Pour the wine over the chicken. Cover and cook for 50 minutes.

Add the olives to the casserole and mix in. Pour in the cream, cover, and return to the oven for 10–20 minutes.

Meanwhile, bring a large pan of lightly salted water to a boil. Add the pasta and the remaining oil and cook for 8–10 minutes or until tender, but still firm to the bite. Drain the pasta well and transfer to a serving dish.

Arrange the chicken on top of the pasta, spoon over the sauce and serve immediately. Alternatively, place the pasta in a large serving bowl and serve separately.

Hot & Spicy Chicken

serves 4

2 tablespoons butter

4 tablespoons olive oil

1 onion, finely chopped

2 garlic cloves, finely chopped

1 tablespoon chopped fresh ginger

1 fresh green chile, seeded and chopped

1 celery stalk, finely chopped

One 14.5-ounce can chopped tomatoes

2 tablespoons tomato paste

Pinch of firmly packed brown sugar, to taste

½ teaspoon ground cumin

½ teaspoon ground coriander

½ teaspoon ground turmeric

½ cup water

1 pound 6 ounces chicken, diced

²/₃ cup heavy cream

1 pound baby spinach

Pinch of salt and freshly ground black pepper

Warm naan, to serve

Melt the butter with half the oil in a pan. Add the onion, garlic, ginger, chile, and celery and cook over low heat, stirring occasionally, for 5 minutes, until softened.

Stir in the tomatoes, tomato paste, sugar to taste, spices, and water and season to taste with salt and pepper. Increase the heat to medium and bring to a boil, then reduce the heat and simmer, stirring occasionally, for 15–20 minutes, until thickened.

Meanwhile, heat the remaining oil in a skillet. Add the chicken and cook over medium heat, stirring frequently, for 5–7 minutes, until lightly browned all over. Remove with a slotted spoon.

Stir the chicken and cream into the sauce and simmer for 6 minutes, until the meat is tender and cooked through.

Add the spinach and cook, stirring constantly, for 2–4 minutes, until wilted. Bring back to a boil, then transfer to a warmed serving dish. Serve immediately with naan.

Chicken Stuffed with Spinach & Garlic

serves 4

4 x 6-ounce part-boned chicken breasts

4 ounces frozen spinach, thawed

¾ cup lowfat ricotta cheese

2 garlic cloves, crushed

1 tablespoon olive oil

1 onion, chopped

1 red bell pepper, seeded and sliced

One 14.5-ounce can chopped tomatoes

6 tablespoons wine or chicken stock

10 stuffed olives, sliced

Pinch of salt

Freshly ground black pepper

Sprigs of fresh flat-leaf parsley, for garnish

Pasta or rice for serving

Preheat the oven to 400°F.

Make a slit between the skin and meat on one side of each chicken breast. Lift the skin to form a pocket, being careful to leave the skin attached to the other side.

Put the spinach into a strainer and press out the water with a spoon. Mix with the ricotta, half the garlic, and the seasoning.

Spoon the spinach mixture under the skin of each chicken breast, then secure the edge of the skin with toothpicks.

Heat the oil in a skillet, add the onion, and cook for a minute, stirring. Add the remaining garlic and the bell pepper and cook for 2 minutes. Stir in the tomatoes, wine, olives, and seasoning. Set the sauce aside and chill the chicken if preparing in advance.

Bring the sauce to a boil, pour into an ovenproof dish, and arrange the chicken breasts on top in a single layer.

Cook, uncovered for about 35 minutes, until the chicken is golden and cooked through. Test by making a slit in one of the chicken breasts with a skewer to make sure the juices run clear.

Spoon a little of the sauce over the chicken breasts, then transfer to serving plates, and garnish with the parsley. Serve with the pasta or rice.

Spiced Chicken & Onion Rice

serves 4

1 tablespoon Chinese five-spice powder

2 tablespoons cornstarch

12 ounces skinless, boneless chicken breast portions, diced

3 tablespoons peanut oil

1 onion, diced

8 ounces long-grain white rice

½ teaspoon ground turmeric

2½ cups chicken stock

2 tablespoons chopped fresh chives

Place the five-spice powder and cornstarch in a large bowl. Add the chicken pieces and toss to coat all over.

Heat 2 tablespoons of the peanut oil in a large preheated wok. Add the chicken to the wok and stir-fry for 5 minutes. Using a slotted spoon, remove the chicken and set aside.

Add the remaining peanut oil to the wok.

Add the onion to the wok and stir-fry for 1 minute.

Add the rice, turmeric, and stock to the wok and gently bring to a boil.

Return the chicken pieces to the wok, reduce the heat, and let simmer gently for about 10 minutes, or until the liquid has been absorbed and the rice is tender.

Add the chives, stir to mix, and serve hot.

Italian Turkey Cutlets

1 tablespoon olive oil

Four 3-4-ounce turkey cutlets

2 red bell peppers, seeded and sliced

1 red onion, sliced

2 garlic cloves, finely chopped

One 14.5-ounce can chopped tomatoes, strained

²/₃ cup medium white wine

1 tablespoon chopped fresh marjoram

Salt and freshly ground pepper, to taste

One 14.5-ounce can cannellini beans, drained and rinsed

3 tablespoons fresh white breadcrumbs

Fresh basil sprigs, to garnish

Heat the oil in a ovenproof casserole. Add the turkey cutlets and cook over medium heat for 5–10 minutes, turning occasionally, until browned all over. Transfer to a plate using a slotted spoon.

Add the bell peppers and onion to the casserole and cook over low heat, stirring occasionally, for 5 minutes, or until softened. Add the garlic and cook for an additional 2 minutes.

Return the turkey to the casserole and add the strained tomatoes, wine, and marjoram. Season to taste with salt and pepper. Bring to a boil, then reduce the heat, cover, and simmer, stirring occasionally, for 25–30 minutes, or until the turkey is cooked through and tender.

Preheat the broiler to medium.

Stir in the cannellini beans. Simmer for an additional 5 minutes. Sprinkle the breadcrumbs over the top and place under the preheated broiler for 2–3 minutes, or until golden. Serve immediately, garnished with basil sprigs.

Artichoke Chicken

serves 4

4 6-ounce chicken breasts, part boned

2 tablespoons butter

2 tablespoons olive oil

2 red onions, cut into wedges

2 tablespoons lemon juice

²/₃ cup dry white wine

²/₃ cup chicken stock

2 teaspoons all-purpose flour

One 14.5-ounce can artichokes drained and halved

Pinch of salt

Freshly ground black pepper

Season the chicken with salt and pepper to taste. Heat the oil and 1 tablespoon of the butter in a large skillet. Add the chicken and fry for 4–5 minutes on each side until lightly golden. Remove from the skillet using a slotted spoon.

Toss the onion in the lemon juice and add to the skillet. Gently fry, stirring, for 3–4 minutes until just beginning to soften.

Return the chicken to the skillet. Pour in the wine and stock, bring to a boil, cover, and simmer gently for 30 minutes.

Remove the chicken from the skillet, reserving the cooking juices, and keep warm. Bring the juices to a boil, and boil rapidly for 5 minutes.

Blend the remaining butter with the flour to form a paste. Reduce the juices to a simmer and spoon the paste into the skillet, stirring until thickened.

Adjust the seasoning according to taste, stir in the artichoke hearts, and cook for an additional 2 minutes. Pour the mixture over the chicken and serve.

Spanish Chicken with Garlic

2–3 tablespoons all-purpose flour

Pinch of cayenne pepper

4 6-ounce chicken pieces

4 tablespoons olive oil

20 large garlic cloves, each halved and cored

1 large bay leaf

2 cups chicken stock

4 tablespoons dry white wine

Pinch of salt

Freshly ground black pepper

Put about 2 tablespoons of the flour in a bag and season with cayenne pepper and salt and pepper to taste. Add a chicken piece and shake until it is lightly coated with the flour, shaking off the excess. Repeat with the remaining pieces, adding more flour and seasoning, if necessary.

Heat 3 tablespoons of the oil in a large skillet. Add the garlic cloves and fry for about 2 minutes, stirring, to flavor the oil. Remove the garlic with a slotted spoon and set aside.

Add the chicken pieces to the skillet, skin side down, and fry for 5 minutes or until the skin is golden brown. Turn and fry for an additional 5 minutes, adding an extra 1–2 tablespoons of oil if necessary.

Return the garlic to the skillet. Add the bay leaf, stock, and wine and bring to a boil. Reduce the heat, cover, and simmer for 25 minutes or until the chicken is tender and the garlic cloves are very soft.

Transfer the chicken to a serving platter and keep warm. Bring the cooking liquid to a boil and boil until reduced to about 1 cup. Adjust the seasoning, if necessary.

Spoon the sauce over the chicken pieces and sprinkle the garlic cloves around it. Garnish with the parsley and serve.

Chicken & Sausage Gumbo

⅓ cup vegetable oil

⅓ cup flour

1 onion, diced

3 ribs celery, diced

2 green bell pepper, seeded, diced

½ cup minced green onions

3 cloves garlic, crushed

1 pound Andouille sausage, or other spicy, smoked sausage, cut in 1-inch pieces

6 cups chicken broth

1 can (10.5-ounce) diced tomatoes with green chilies

1½ pounds boneless, skinless chicken thighs, cut in 2-inch pieces

1 tablespoon Cajun seasoning

1 teaspoon salt

¼ teaspoon cayenne pepper, or to taste

½ teaspoon black pepper

2 cups frozen cut okra, thawed, drained

1 pound shrimp, peeled, deveined

To make the roux: In a heavy Dutch oven or pot, cook the oil and flour over medium low heat, stirring with a wooden spoon, until it's a light, nutty brown color.

Add the onion, celery, and bell pepper to the roux and cook for another 5 minutes to soften the vegetables. Add the green onions, garlic, and sausage; stir, and cook for 3 minutes.

Add the broth, tomatoes, chicken, Cajun seasoning, salt, cayenne pepper, and black pepper. Bring to a boil, reduce to low, and simmer, stirring occasionally, for 1 hour. Stir in the okra and simmer for another 30 minutes, or until the chicken is very tender.

Stir in the shrimp and cook for 3 to 4 minutes, or until they're cooked through. Taste for salt and spice, and adjust seasoning if needed. Serve hot with cooked long-grain rice.

Chicken & White Bean Chili

2 pounds boneless, skinless chicken thigh, cut into 1-inch pieces

2 tablespoons vegetable oil

1 onion, diced

3 cloves garlic, minced

1 teaspoon salt

2 tablespoons ground cumin

½ teaspoon ground chipotle pepper

¼ teaspoon cinnamon

½ teaspoon fresh ground black pepper

1 red bell pepper, seeded, diced

1 green bell pepper, seeded, diced

1 jalapeno pepper, seeded, diced

1 (10.5-ounce) can diced tomatoes with green chilies

3 cups chicken broth, more as needed

2 (14.5-ounce) cans white kidney beans, great northern, or navy beans, drained

Cayenne pepper to taste

Chopped fresh cilantro to garnish, optional

Add oil to a large, heavy pot over medium-high heat. When the oil is hot, add the chunks of chicken, and sauté for 5 minutes. Add the onions, garlic, and salt; cook, stirring, for another 2 minutes. Add the cumin, chipotle, cinnamon, and fresh ground black pepper; cook, stirring, for another minute.

Add the red bell pepper, green bell pepper, jalapeno pepper, diced tomato with green chilies, and chicken broth. Bring to a simmer, turn heat to low, and cook, stirring occasionally, for 30 minutes.

Stir in the beans and simmer another 30 minutes. Taste and adjust for salt and pepper. Serve hot with a shake of cayenne and cilantro if desired.

Chicken Parmesan Casserole with Tomato Sauce

serves 6

6 (6-7 ounce) boneless, skinless chicken breasts

Salt and freshly ground black pepper, to taste

2 tablespoons olive oil

2 cloves garlic, minced

4 cups marinara sauce (see recipe)

¼ cup chopped basil

1 cup shredded mozzarella

½ cup grated Parmesan

1 (5 ounce) package garlic croutons

For The Marinara Sauce

¼ cup olive oil

1 onion, diced

1 rib celery, finely dice

4 cloves garlic, minced

1 teaspoon salt

2 teaspoons sugar

½ teaspoon dried Italian herbs

Pinch of red pepper flakes

1 teaspoon anchovy paste

1 teaspoon white wine vinegar

1 tablespoon tomato paste

2 (14.5-ounce) cans whole peeled plum tomatoes, coarsely pureed

2 tablespoons chopped fresh basil

Preheat oven to 350°F.

Season the chicken breasts with salt and pepper. Set aside. Spread the olive oil, garlic, and red pepper flakes evenly on the bottom of a 9 x 13-inch casserole dish. Add 1 cup of the marinara sauce, and spread evenly.

Place the chicken breasts in the dish, and space evenly. Top with the rest of the marinara sauce, basil and half the mozzarella and Parmesan cheeses. Sprinkle the croutons evenly over the chicken, then top with the remaining cheeses.

Bake for 40 minutes, or until the top is browned and the chicken is cooked through. Let rest before serving.

To make the marinara sauce: In a saucepan, sauté the onions and celery in the olive oil for 5 to 6 minutes, or until translucent. Add the garlic and cook for 1 minute more. Add the salt, sugar, dried herbs, pepper flakes, anchovy paste, vinegar, and tomato paste. Cook, stirring, for 2 minutes. Add the tomatoes, bring to a simmer, turn down to low and simmer gently, stirring occasionally, for 45 minutes. Add water if necessary, to adjust thickness. Adjust the seasoning to taste, and reserve.

Fried Chicken with Tomato & Bacon Sauce

serves 4

2 tablespoons butter

2 tablespoons olive oil

4 skinless, boneless chicken breasts or 8 skinless, boneless chicken thighs

Tomato & Bacon Sauce

2 tablespoons butter

2 tablespoons olive oil

1 large onion, finely chopped

2 garlic cloves, finely chopped

1 celery stalk, finely chopped

4 slices bacon, chopped

One 14.5-ounce can chopped tomatoes

2 tablespoons tomato paste

Pinch of firmly packed brown sugar, to taste

½ cup water

1 tablespoon chopped fresh basil

1 tablespoon chopped fresh parsley, plus extra to garnish

Salt and pepper

To make the sauce: Melt the butter with the oil in a large pan. Add the onion, garlic, celery, and bacon and cook over low heat, stirring occasionally, for 5 minutes, until softened. Stir in the tomatoes, tomato paste, sugar to taste, and water and season with salt and pepper.

Increase the heat to medium and bring to a boil, then reduce the heat and simmer, stirring occasionally, for 15–20 minutes, until thickened.

Meanwhile, melt the butter with the oil in a large skillet. Add the chicken and cook over medium– high heat for 4–5 minutes on each side, until evenly browned.

Stir the basil and parsley into the sauce. Add the chicken and spoon the sauce over it. Cover and simmer for 10–15 minutes, until cooked through and tender.

Garnish with parsley and serve immediately.

King Ranch Chicken Casserole

1 cup of chicken broth

1 (10.5-ounce) can cream of mushroom soup

1 (10.5-ounce) can cream of chicken soup

1 (10.5-ounce) can diced tomatoes with green chilies

2 tablespoons sour cream

1 white onion, diced small

1 red bell pepper, diced

1 green bell pepper, diced

2 jalapeños, seeded, diced fine, optional

2 teaspoons chile powder

2 teaspoons cumin

1½ teaspoons salt

½ teaspoon dried oregano

½ teaspoon chipotle chile powder

One (4 to 5-pound) cooked chicken, roughly shredded

1 cup grated sharp cheddar cheese

8 to 10 corn tortillas, quartered

Preheat oven to 350°F.

Combine the chicken broth, soups, tomatoes, sour cream, onions, peppers, and spices in a mixing bowl and stir to combine thoroughly. Once mixed, spoon ½ cup of the sauce into a separate bowl and reserve for the top of the casserole dish.

Place half the chicken in a lightly oiled 9 x 13-inch casserole dish. Spoon over half the sauce mixture, and spread evenly. Top with a third of the cheese. Top with half the tortillas. There is no need to overlap the tortilla pieces; a single layer is fine.

Top with the rest of the chicken, and then spread over the rest of the sauce. Top with the next third of the cheese, then the rest of the tortillas to cover the surface completely. Use a spatula to spread over the ½ cup of reserved sauce. Top with the last third of the cheese.

Bake uncovered for 40 minutes, or until golden brown and bubbly. Let rest for 15 minutes before serving.

Chicken Cacciatore

serves 4

2 tablespoons olive oil

8 large chicken thighs (about 3½ pounds)

Salt and freshly ground black pepper

1 large onion, sliced

1½ cups fresh mushrooms, thickly sliced

1 tablespoon flour

½ cup white wine

1½ cup chicken broth

1 cup chopped tomato

8 cloves garlic, peeled (left whole)

3 springs fresh rosemary

1 bay leaf

1 teaspoon dried oregano

½ teaspoon red pepper flakes,

1 teaspoon salt

1 red bell pepper, seeded, sliced

1 green bell pepper, seeded, sliced

Preheat oven to 350°F.

Season the chicken generously with salt and freshly ground black pepper. Place a heavy Dutch oven on the stove over a medium-high heat; add the olive oil and brown the chicken thighs well on all both sides.

Remove the chicken, and add the onions and mushrooms. Reduce the heat to medium and sauté for about 5 minutes, until the onions soften.

Stir in the flour and cook for one minute. Stir in the wine, tomato, and chicken broth; bring to a boil, scraping the bottom with a wooden spoon to release the caramelized bits.

Add the garlic, cloves, rosemary, bay leaf, oregano, pepper flakes, and salt. Stir to combine.

Place the chicken pieces, and any juices, over the sauce, and top with the sliced peppers. Cover with the lid and place in oven for 45 minutes. Remove the lid and roast for 15 minutes more.

Remove from oven and let rest, covered, for 10 minutes. Skim any excess fat from the top of the sauce. Taste and adjust seasoning. Serve over pasta, rice, or polenta.

Stir-fried Turkey with Cranberry Glaze

serves 4

1 pound boneless turkey breast

2 tablespoons vegetable oil

2 tablespoons preserved ginger, drained and finely chopped

½ cup fresh or frozen cranberries

½ cup canned chestnuts

4 tablespoons cranberry sauce

3 tablespoons light soy sauce

Salt and freshly ground pepper, to taste

Remove any skin from the turkey breast and, using a sharp knife, thinly slice the meat.

Heat the oil in a large preheated wok or heavy skillet. Add the slices of turkey to the wok or skillet and stir-fry over medium heat for about 5 minutes, or until cooked through.

Add the preserved ginger and the cranberries to the wok or skillet and cook for 2–3 minutes, or until the cranberries start to become soft. Add the chestnuts, cranberry sauce, and soy sauce, season to taste with salt and pepper, and bubble for 2–3 minutes.

Transfer the glazed turkey stir-fry to warmed individual serving dishes and serve immediately.

Chicken Casserole with Herb Crust

4 whole (drumstick and thigh) chicken legs, dusted in flour

1 tablespoon olive oil

1 tablespoon butter

1 onion, chopped

3 garlic cloves, sliced

4 parsnips, peeled and cut into large chunks

1 cup dry white wine

3½ cups chicken broth

3 leeks, white parts only, trimmed, sliced

3 ounces prunes, halved (optional)

1 tablespoon Dijon mustard

1 tablespoon mixed dried herbs

Salt and freshly ground pepper, to taste

1 cup fresh bread crumbs

½ cup feta cheese, crumbled

2 tablespoons chopped fresh tarragon

2 tablespoons chopped fresh Italian parsley

Preheat oven to 350°F.

In a Dutch oven or flameproof casserole dish, melt the olive oil and butter together, then fry the chicken until it is golden brown. Remove with a slotted spoon and keep warm.

Add the onion, garlic, and parsnips to the casserole and cook until the vegetables are slightly browned. Add the wine, chicken broth, leeks, prunes if using), mustard, and mixed herbs and season with salt and pepper to taste. Return the chicken to the casserole, cover, and cook in the oven for 1 hour.

Mix the breadcrumbs, feta cheese, and herbs together in a bowl.

Remove the casserole from the oven and increase the oven temperature to 400°F. Sprinkle the bread crumb mixture over the chicken, and return the casserole to the oven, uncovered, for 10 minutes or until the crust starts to brown slightly. Remove from the oven and serve immediately.

Mexican Turkey

serves 4

6 tablespoons all-purpose flour

Salt and freshly ground pepper, to taste

4 turkey breast fillets

3 tablespoons vegetable oil

1 onion, thinly sliced

1 red bell pepper, seeded and sliced

1¼ cups chicken stock

2 tablespoons raisins

4 tomatoes, peeled, seeded, and chopped

1 teaspoon chili powder

½ teaspoon ground cinnamon

Pinch of ground cumin

1 ounce semisweet chocolate, finely chopped or grated

Sprigs of fresh cilantro, to garnish

Preheat the oven to 325°F.

Spread the flour on a plate and season with salt and pepper. Coat the turkey fillets in the seasoned flour, shaking off any excess.

Heat the oil in a large ovenproof casserole. Add the turkey fillets and cook over medium heat, turning occasionally, for 5–10 minutes, or until golden. Transfer to a plate with a slotted spoon.

Add the onion and bell pepper to the casserole. Cook over low heat, stirring occasionally, for 5 minutes, or until softened. Sprinkle in any remaining seasoned flour and cook, stirring constantly, for 1 minute.

Gradually stir in the stock, then add the raisins, chopped tomatoes, chili powder, cinnamon, cumin, and chocolate. Season to taste with salt and pepper. Bring to a boil, stirring constantly.

Return the turkey to the casserole, cover, and cook in the preheated oven for 50 minutes. Serve immediately, garnished with sprigs of cilantro.

Chicken Pot Pie

serves 6

1 tablespoon olive oil

1½ cups white button mushrooms, sliced

1 onion, diced

3 large carrots, sliced

2 sticks celery, sliced

4 cups cold chicken broth

6 tablespoons butter

½ cup all-purpose flour

2 pounds skinless, boneless chicken breasts, cut in 1-inch cubes

1 cup frozen green peas

1 teaspoon chopped fresh thyme leaves or a pinch of dried

1 teaspoon salt

¼ teaspoon black pepper

1½ pounds pie dough (enough for 2 x 10 inch pies)

1 egg, beaten

Preheat oven to 400°F. In a large saucepan, sauté the mushrooms and onions in the olive oil over medium heat until golden. Add the carrots, celery, and 2 cups of chicken broth. Bring to a boil, reduce to low and simmer until the vegetables are almost tender.

Melt the butter in a large saucepan over medium heat. Whisk in the flour and cook, stirring, for 4 minutes, or until the flour is a light tan color and smells like cooked piecrust. Slowly whisk in 2 cups of cold chicken broth. Simmer over medium-low heat until the mixture thickens. Remove from heat, and reserve.

Add the vegetables and broth from the other pan when ready, and stir to combine. Add the chicken, peas, thyme, salt and pepper. Bring back to a simmer and cook, stirring, for 5 minutes. Taste for seasoning and set aside until needed.

Divide the pot pie filling among 6 large (15-ounce) ramekins (fill to ½ inch from the top). Cut out circles of pie dough 1 inch larger than the width of the ramekins. Place the dough over the pot pies. Go around each piece of dough, folding a ½ inch over to form a rim. If desired, pinch with your finger tips to form a crimped edge. Cut a small "X" in the center of each crust.

Place the ramekins on a sheet pan. Brush the tops with the beaten egg. Bake for 35 to 40 minutes, or until pies are golden brown and bubbly. Cool for 15 minutes before serving.

Spicy Aromatic Chicken

serves 4

One 3 to 4-pound chicken, cut into 8 pieces, skinned

½ lemon, cut into wedges

4 tablespoons olive oil

1 onion, chopped coarsely

2 large garlic cloves, chopped finely

½ cup dry white wine

One 14.5-ounce can chopped tomatoes, with their juice

Pinch of sugar

½ teaspoon ground cinnamon

½ teaspoon ground cloves

½ teaspoon ground allspice

One 14.5-ounce can or jar of artichoke hearts, drained

8 black olives, pitted

Salt and freshly ground pepper, to taste

Rub the chicken pieces with the lemon. Heat the oil in a large ovenproof casserole or lidded skillet. Add the onion and garlic and sauté for 5 minutes, until softened. Add the chicken pieces and fry for 5–10 minutes, until browned on all sides.

Pour in the wine and add the tomatoes with their juice, the sugar, cinnamon, cloves, allspice, salt and pepper to taste, and bring to a boil. Cover the casserole and simmer for 45 minutes to 1 hour, until the chicken is tender.

Meanwhile, if using artichoke hearts, cut them in half. Add the artichokes and the olives to the casserole 10 minutes before the end of cooking, and continue to simmer until heated through. Serve hot.

Chicken, Tomato & Onion Casserole

serves 4

1½ tablespoons unsalted butter

2 tablespoons olive oil

One 4-pound chicken, skinned, bone in and cut into 8 pieces

2 red onions, sliced

2 garlic cloves, finely chopped

One 14.5-ounce can tomatoes, chopped

2 tablespoons chopped fresh Italian parsley

6 fresh basil leaves, torn

1 tablespoon sun-dried tomato paste

⅔ cup red wine

Salt and freshly ground pepper, to taste

1½ cups small mushrooms, sliced

Preheat the oven to 325°F.

Melt the butter with the olive oil in a Dutch oven or casserole dish. Add the chicken pieces and fry, turning frequently for about 10 minutes, or until golden brown. Using a slotted spoon, transfer the chicken pieces to a platter.

Add the onions and garlic to the dish and cook over low heat, stirring occasionally, for 10 minutes, or until the onions become translucent. Add the tomatoes with their juice, the parsley, basil leaves, tomato paste, and wine, and season to taste with salt and pepper. Bring to a boil, then return the chicken pieces to the casserole, pushing them down into the sauce.

Cover and cook in a preheated oven for 50 minutes. Add the mushrooms and cook for an additional 10 minutes, until the mushrooms are warmed through. Serve immediately.

2

Meats

Pepper Pot Stew

serves 4

1 pound braising beef, such as chuck or round

1½ tablespoons all-purpose flour

2 tablespoons olive oil

1 red onion, chopped

3–4 garlic cloves, crushed

1 fresh green chile, seeded and chopped

3 celery ribs, sliced

4 whole cloves

1 teaspoons ground allspice

1–2 teaspoons hot pepper sauce

2½ cups beef stock

1 small winter squash, such as acorn, peeled, seeded, and cut into small chunks

1 large red bell pepper, seeded and chopped

4 tomatoes, coarsely chopped

10 pieces okra, trimmed and halved

Mixed wild and basmati rice, to serve

Trim any fat or gristle from the beef and cut into 1-inch chunks. Toss the beef in the flour until well coated and reserve any remaining flour.

Heat the oil in a large, heavy-bottom pan and cook the onion, garlic, chile, and celery with the cloves and allspice, stirring frequently, for 5 minutes, or until softened. Add the beef and cook over high heat, stirring frequently, for 3 minutes, or until browned on all sides and sealed. Sprinkle in the reserved flour and cook, stirring constantly, for 2 minutes, then remove from the heat.

Add the hot pepper sauce and gradually stir in the stock, then return to the heat and bring to a boil, stirring. Reduce the heat, then cover and simmer, stirring occasionally, for 1½ hours.

Add the squash and red bell pepper to the pan and simmer for an additional 15 minutes. Add the tomatoes and okra and simmer for an additional 15 minutes, or until the beef is tender. Serve with mixed wild and basmati rice.

Pot Roast with Potatoes & Dill

serves 6

2½ tablespoons all-purpose flour

1 teaspoon salt

¼ teaspoon pepper

1 rolled brisket of beef, weighing 3 pounds 8 ounces

2 tablespoons vegetable oil

2 tablespoons butter

1 onion, finely chopped

2 celery stalks, diced

2 carrots, peeled and diced

1 teaspoon dill seeds

1 teaspoon dried thyme or oregano

1½ cups red wine

⅔–1 cup beef stock

4–5 potatoes, cut into large chunks and boiled until just tender

2 tablespoons chopped fresh dill, to serve

Preheat the oven to 275°F.

Mix 2 tablespoons of the flour with the salt and pepper in a shallow dish. Dip the meat to coat. Heat the oil in a flameproof casserole and brown the meat all over. Transfer to a plate. Add half the butter to the casserole and cook the onion, celery, carrots, dill seeds, and thyme for 5 minutes. Return the meat and juices to the casserole.

Pour in the wine and enough stock to reach one-third of the way up the meat. Bring to a boil, cover, and cook in the oven for 3 hours, turning the meat every 30 minutes. After it has been cooking for 2 hours, add the potatoes and more stock if necessary.

When ready, transfer the meat and vegetables to a warmed serving dish. Strain the cooking liquid to remove any solids, then return the liquid to the casserole.

Mix the remaining butter and flour to a paste. Bring the cooking liquid to a boil. Whisk in small pieces of the flour and butter paste, whisking constantly until the sauce is smooth. Pour the sauce over the meat and vegetables. Sprinkle with the fresh dill to serve.

Pork & Beans

7 ounces dried cannelloni beans, soaked in cold water overnight

Olive oil, for frying

1 pound 5 ounces boneless leg of pork, cut into 2-inch chunks

1 large onion, sliced

3 large garlic cloves, crushed

One 14.5-ounce can chopped tomatoes

2 green bell peppers, seeded and sliced

Finely grated rind of 1 large orange

Pinch of salt

Freshly ground black pepper

2 tablespoons fresh parsley, for garnish

Preheat the oven to 350°F.

Drain the cannellini beans and put in a large pan with fresh water to cover. Bring to a boil and boil rapidly for 10 minutes. Reduce the heat and simmer for 20 minutes. Drain and set aside.

Add enough oil to cover the base of a skillet in a very thin layer. Heat the oil over medium heat, add a few pieces of the pork, and fry on all sides until brown. Remove from the skillet and set aside. Repeat with the remaining pork.

Add 1 tablespoon of the oil to the skillet, add the onion and cook for 3 minutes. Stir in the garlic and cook for an additional 2 minutes. Return the pork to the skillet.

Add the tomatoes and bring to a boil. Reduce the heat and stir in the bell pepper slices, orange rind, and drained beans. Season with salt and pepper to taste.

Transfer the contents of the skillet to a casserole. Cover the casserole and cook for 45 minutes until the beans and pork are both tender. Sprinkle with the parsley and serve immediately, straight from the casserole.

Beef Goulash

2 tablespoons vegetable oil

1 large onion, chopped

1 garlic clove, crushed

1 pound 10 ounces lean beef

2 tablespoons paprika

One 14.5-ounce can chopped tomatoes

2 tablespoons tomato paste

1 large red bell pepper, seeded and chopped

1 cup small mushrooms, sliced

2 cups beef stock

1 tablespoon cornstarch

1 tablespoon water

4 tablespoons lowfat plain yogurt

Pinch of paprika for sprinkling

Pinch of salt

Freshly ground pepper

2 tablespoons chopped fresh parsley, for garnish

2 cups long-grain rice, for serving

Heat the oil in a large skillet and cook the onion and garlic for 3–4 minutes.

Cut the beef into chunks and cook over high heat for 3 minutes until browned all over. Add the paprika and stir well, then add the chopped tomatoes, tomato paste, bell pepper, and mushrooms. Cook for 2 minutes, stirring frequently.

Pour in the stock. Bring to a boil and then reduce the heat. Cover and simmer for 1½–2 hours until the meat is tender.

Blend the cornstarch with the water, then add to the skillet, stirring until thickened and smooth. Cook for 1 minute, then season with salt and pepper to taste.

Put the yogurt in a serving bowl and sprinkle with a little paprika.

Transfer the beef goulash to a warmed serving dish, garnish with the parsley and serve with the rice and paprika yogurt.

Lamb Stew with Chickpeas

serves 4

6 tablespoons olive oil

8 ounces chorizo sausage, cut into ¼-inch slices, casings removed

2 large onions, chopped

6 large garlic cloves, crushed

2 pound boned leg of lamb, cut into 2-inch chunks

1¼ cups lamb stock or water

½ cup red wine

2 tablespoons sherry vinegar

Two 10.5-ounce cans chopped tomatoes

4 sprigs fresh thyme, plus extra

To Garnish

2 bay leaves

½ teaspoon sweet Spanish paprika

Two 14-ounce cans chickpeas, rinsed and drained

Salt and pepper

Preheat the oven to 325°F.

Heat 4 tablespoons of the oil in a large, heavy-bottom flameproof casserole over medium-high heat. Reduce the heat, add the chorizo, and cook for 1 minute; set aside. Add the onions to the casserole and cook for 2 minutes, then add the garlic and continue cooking for 3 minutes, or until the onions are soft, but not brown. Remove from the casserole and set aside.

Heat the remaining 2 tablespoons of oil in the casserole. Add the lamb chunks in a single layer without overcrowding the casserole, and cook until browned on all sides; work in batches, if necessary.

Return the onion mixture to the casserole with all the lamb. Stir in the stock, wine, vinegar, tomatoes with their juices, and salt and pepper to taste. Bring to a boil, scraping any glazed bits from the bottom of the casserole. Reduce the heat and stir in the thyme, bay leaves, and paprika.

Transfer to oven and cook, covered, for 40–45 minutes until the lamb is tender. Stir in the chickpeas and return to the oven, uncovered, for 10 minutes, or until they are heated through and the juices are reduced.

Taste and adjust the seasoning. Garnish with thyme and serve.

Spicy Pork with Prunes

3 pound pork joint, such as leg or shoulder

Juice of 2–3 limes

10 garlic cloves, chopped

3–4 tablespoons mild chili powder

4 tablespoons vegetable oil

2 onions, chopped

2¼ cups chicken stock

25 small tomatoes, roughly chopped

25 prunes, pitted

1 teaspoon sugar

Pinch of ground cinnamon

Pinch of ground allspice

Pinch of ground cumin

Pinch of salt

Warmed tortillas, for serving

Preheat the oven to 350°F.

Combine the pork with the lime juice, garlic, chili powder, 2 tablespoons of the oil, and salt. Set aside to marinate in the refrigerator overnight.

Remove the pork from the marinade. Wipe the pork dry with paper towels and reserve the marinade. Heat the remaining oil in a flameproof casserole and brown the pork evenly until just golden. Add the onions, the reserved marinade, and stock. Cover and cook for about 2–3 hours until tender.

Spoon off the fat from the surface of the cooking liquid and add the tomatoes. Continue to cook for about 20 minutes until the tomatoes are tender. Mash the tomatoes into a coarse purée. Add the prunes and sugar, then adjust the seasoning, adding cinnamon, allspice, and cumin to taste, as well as extra chili powder, if wished.

Increase the oven temperature to 400°F and return the meat and sauce to the oven for an additional 20–30 minutes or until the meat has browned on top and the juices have thickened.

Remove the meat and set aside for a few minutes. Carefully carve it into thin slices and spoon the sauce over the top. Serve warm with the tortillas.

Beef in Beer

Few sprigs of fresh parsley

1 tablespoon vegetable oil

1 pound lean beef, trimmed and cut into 1-inch cubes

1 onion, chopped

2 cups small mushrooms, sliced

1 tablespoon firmly packed brown sugar

1½ cups beef stock

1¼ cups dark beer or stout

Pinch of salt

Freshly ground black pepper

Using a sharp knife, finely chop the parsley and set aside until required.

Heat the oil in a large, heavy-bottom skillet. Add the beef and cook, stirring frequently, for 10 minutes, or until browned all over. Using a slotted spoon, transfer the meat to a large ovenproof casserole dish.

Add the onion to the skillet and cook over low heat, stirring occasionally, for 3 minutes. Add the mushrooms and sugar and cook, stirring occasionally, for 10 minutes. Transfer to the casserole with a slotted spoon.

Add the stock, beer, and reserved parsley to the casserole and season with salt and pepper to taste. Bring to a boil, cover, and let simmer over very low heat for 1½–2 hours, or until tender. Serve immediately.

Red Curry Pork with Peppers

serves 4

2 tablespoons vegetable oil

1 onion, coarsely chopped

2 garlic cloves, chopped

1 pound pork tenderloin, thickly sliced

1 red bell pepper, seeded and sliced

1 cup small mushrooms, quartered

2 tablespoons red curry paste

4-ounce block creamed coconut, chopped

1¼ cups pork stock or vegetable stock

2 tablespoons soy sauce

4 tomatoes, peeled, seeded, and chopped

Handful of fresh cilantro, chopped

4 cups freshly cooked rice, to serve

Heat the oil in a wok or large skillet and sauté the onion and garlic for 1–2 minutes, until they are softened but not browned.

Add the pork slices and stir-fry for 2–3 minutes, until browned all over. Add the bell pepper, mushrooms, and curry paste.

Dissolve the coconut in the stock and add to the wok with the soy sauce. Bring to a boil and then simmer for 4–5 minutes until the liquid has reduced and thickened.

Add the tomatoes and cilantro and cook for 1–2 minutes, before serving with the cooked rice.

Braised Lamb Shanks

serves 6

6 lamb shanks, about 5½ pounds

2 tablespoons olive oil

½ teaspoon dried rosemary

½ teaspoon dried thyme

Salt and fresh ground black pepper to taste

1 tablespoon butter

1 onion, diced

1 rib celery, diced

1 large carrot, diced

1 tablespoon flour

4 cloves garlic, minced

½ cup drinkable red wine

1 cup chicken broth

1 tbsp balsamic vinegar

½ cup water

⅛ teaspoon cinnamon

1 teaspoon minced fresh rosemary leaves

Pre-heat oven to 450°F. Place the shanks in a deep, 15 x 10 inch baking dish, or similar sized roasting pan, large enough to fit the shanks in one layer. Rub with the olive oil, dried rosemary and thyme. Season generously with salt and pepper on both sides. Roast for 30 minutes to brown the lamb.

While the lamb is browning, place a saucepan on medium-high heat, and add the butter. When the butter foams, add the onion, celery, and carrot. Cook for about 6 to 7 minutes, or until the vegetables soften and the edges start to brown and caramelize.

Stir in the flour and cook for 1 minute. Add the garlic and cook for 1 minute more. Stir in the wine. When the wine comes to a boil, stir in the chicken broth, balsamic vinegar, water, and cinnamon. Bring back to a boil, turn off and reserve.

When the lamb has finished browning, remove, and turn the oven down to 325°F. Pour over the sauce mixture, and distribute evenly. Cover with heavy-duty foil, crimping the edges to form a tight seal. Roast for 1 hour, lift the foil, turn over the shanks, rewrap and cook for 1 more hour, or until fork tender. Remove the lamb shanks to a large bowl, and cover with foil to keep warm.

Pour the braising liquid into a saucepan, and boil on high heat for 10 minutes, or until reduced by half and slight thickened. As the sauce reduces, the excess fat will pool up in the center of the pan and should be skimmed off with a ladle. Add the fresh rosemary, taste and adjust for seasoning. Transfer the lamb shanks to a serving platter, and serve topped with the sauce.

Beef in Red Wine

serves 6

4 tablespoons all-purpose flour

Salt and freshly ground black pepper, to taste

2¼ pounds lean braising beef, such as chuck or round, diced

6 slices bacon, diced

4 tablespoons olive oil

3 tablespoons butter

16 pearl onions or shallots

3 garlic cloves, finely chopped

1½ cups sliced mushrooms

2½ cups full-bodied red wine

¾ cup beef stock

1 tablespoon dried mixed herbs

Mashed potatoes, to serve

Fresh Italian parsley sprigs, to garnish

Preheat the oven to 325°F.

Season the flour with salt and pepper to taste and toss the beef in it to coat. Shake off any excess.

Heat a large, ovenproof casserole dish, add the bacon, and cook over medium heat, stirring frequently, for 5 minutes, until golden brown. Remove with a slotted spoon. Heat the oil in the casserole. Add the beef, in batches, and cook, stirring frequently, for 8–10 minutes, until browned all over. Remove with a slotted spoon.

Melt the butter in the casserole, then add the onions and garlic, and cook, stirring frequently, for 5 minutes, until light golden brown. Add the mushrooms and cook, stirring occasionally, for an additional 5 minutes.

Return the beef and bacon to the casserole, pour in the wine and stock, add the dried mixed herbs and bring to a boil. Cover and transfer the casserole to the preheated oven. Cook, stirring 2–3 times, for 1¾–2 hours, until the beef is tender.

Taste and adjust the seasoning, adding salt and pepper if needed. Serve immediately with mashed potatoes, garnished with parsley sprigs.

Garlic Pork & Noodles

serves 4

8 ounces medium egg noodles

3 tablespoons vegetable oil

2 garlic cloves, crushed

12 ounces pork tenderloin, cut into strips

4 ounces small shrimp

1 bunch scallions, finely chopped

¾ cup chopped roasted and shelled unsalted peanuts

3 tablespoons fish sauce

2 teaspoons firmly packed brown sugar

1-2 small red chiles, seeded and finely chopped (to taste)

3 tablespoons lime juice

3 tablespoons chopped fresh cilantro

Place the noodles in a large pan of boiling water, then immediately remove from the heat. Cover and let stand for 6 minutes, stirring once halfway through the time. After 6 minutes the noodles will be perfectly cooked. Alternatively, follow the instructions on the packet. Drain and keep warm.

Heat the oil in a wok, add the garlic and pork, and stir-fry until the pork strips are browned, about 2–3 minutes.

Add the shrimp, scallions, peanuts, fish sauce, sugar, chiles to taste, and lime juice. Stir-fry for an additional minute.

Add the cooked noodles and the cilantro and stir-fry until heated through, about 1 minute. Serve the stir-fry immediately.

"Chili Verde" Green Pork Stew

serves 4

2 tablespoons vegetable oil

4 pounds boneless pork shoulder, cut into 2-inch cubes

Salt and pepper to taste

1 yellow onion, chopped

2 Anaheim chilies, seeded, diced

4 cups (two 16-ounce jars) green salsa (look for one with tomatillos as the main ingredient)

2 teaspoons ground cumin

1 teaspoon dried oregano

1 teaspoon sugar

½ teaspoon chipotle pepper

Sour cream and chopped cilantro to garnish, optional

Season the pork cubes with salt and pepper. In a heavy Dutch oven, heat the oil on medium-high, and sear the pork in batches until very well browned. Reserve the cooked pork in a bowl.

Reduce the heat to medium and add the onions. Sauté until golden, about 5 minutes.

Add the rest of the ingredients, bring to a boil, reduce heat to low, cover, and simmer gently for 1½ to 2 hours, stirring occasionally, or until the pork is very tender. Taste and adjust seasoning.

Serve in bowls topped with sour cream and cilantro.

Beef in Beer with Herb Dumplings

2 tablespoons vegetable oil

2 large onions, thinly sliced

8 carrots, sliced

4 tablespoons all-purpose flour

3 pound braising beef, cut into cubes

1¾ cups stout or dark beer

2 teaspoons firmly packed light brown sugar

2 bay leaves

1 tablespoon chopped fresh thyme

Salt and pepper

Herb Dumplings

¾ cup self-rising flour

Pinch of salt

½ cup lard, chilled and cut into small pieces

2 tablespoon chopped fresh parsley, plus extra to garnish

4 tablespoons water

Preheat the oven to 325°F.

Heat the oil in a flameproof casserole dish. Add the onions and carrots and cook over low heat, stirring occasionally, for 5 minutes, or until the onions are softened. Meanwhile, place the flour in a plastic bag and season with salt and pepper. Add the braising beef to the bag, tie the top, and shake well to coat. Do this in batches, if necessary.

Remove the vegetables from the casserole with a slotted spoon and reserve. Add the braising beef to the casserole, in batches, and cook, stirring frequently, until browned all over. Return all the meat and the onions and carrots to the casserole and sprinkle in any remaining seasoned flour. Pour in the stout and add the sugar, bay leaves, and thyme. Bring to a boil, cover, and transfer to the preheated oven to bake for 1¾ hours.

To make the herb dumplings: Sift the flour and salt into a bowl. Stir in the lard and parsley and add enough of the water to make a soft dough. Shape into small balls between the palms of your hands. Add to the casserole and return to the oven for 30 minutes. Remove and discard the bay leaves and serve, sprinkled with parsley.

Chorizo & Mushroom Pasta

1 pound 8 ounces fresh or dried pasta, such as vermicelli

½ cup olive oil

2 garlic cloves

4 ounces chorizo, sliced

1½ cups wild mushrooms. sliced

3 fresh red chiles, chopped

2 tablespoons freshly grated Parmesan cheese

Pinch of salt

Freshly ground black pepper

Bring a large pan of lightly salted water to a boil. Add the pasta and 1 tablespoon of the oil and cook for 8–10 minutes or until just tender, but still firm to the bite.

Drain the pasta thoroughly, place on a large warmed serving plate, and keep warm.

Meanwhile, heat the remaining oil in a large skillet. Add the garlic and fry for 1 minute.

Add the chorizo and wild mushrooms and cook for 4 minutes. Add the chopped chiles and cook for an additional minute.

Pour the chorizo and wild mushroom mixture over the vermicelli and season with a little salt and pepper.

Sprinkle with the cheese and serve immediately.

Spicy Pork & Rice

10 ounces long-grain white rice

2½ cups cold water

1 pound pork tenderloin sliced

2 teaspoons Chinese five-spice powder

4 tablespoons cornstarch

3 large eggs, beaten

2 tablespoons firmly packed brown sugar

2 tablespoons sunflower oil

1 onion, diced

2 cloves garlic, crushed

2 large carrots, diced

1 red bell pepper, seeded and diced

1 cup peas

2 tablespoons butter

Pinch of salt

Rinse the rice under cold running water. Place the rice in a large pan, and add the cold water and a pinch of salt. Bring to a boil, cover, then reduce the heat and let simmer for about 9 minutes, or until all of the liquid has been absorbed and the rice is tender.

Meanwhile, slice the pork into very thin even-size pieces, using a sharp knife.

Set the pork strips aside until required.

Whisk together the five-spice powder, cornstarch, 1 egg, and the sugar. Toss the pork in the mixture until coated.

Heat the oil in a large wok or skillet. Add the pork and cook over high heat until the pork is cooked through and crispy. Remove the pork from the wok with a slotted spoon and set aside until required.

Add the onion, garlic, carrots, bell pepper, and peas to the wok and stir-fry for 5 minutes.

Return the pork to the wok together with the cooked rice and stir-fry for 5 minutes.

Heat the butter in a skillet. Add the remaining beaten eggs and cook until set. Turn out onto a clean board and slice thinly. Toss the strips of egg into the rice mixture and serve immediately.

Beef Casserole with Mashed Potatoes

serves 2

2 teaspoons vegetable oil

8 ounces extra-lean braising beef, cut into 8 pieces

10 small shallots

1 garlic clove, crushed

1 tomato, chopped

1½ cups sliced mushrooms

⅔ cup red wine

½ cup chicken broth

1 tablespoon dried mixed herbs

2 bay leaves

2 Idaho potatoes, peeled and sliced

1½–2 tablespoons warm milk

1 teaspoon Dijon mustard

Salt and freshly ground pepper, to taste

1 teaspoon cornstarch

Preheat the oven to 350°F.

Heat the oil in a ovenproof casserole dish. Add the meat and shallots and cook over high heat, stirring, for 4–5 minutes, until the meat is browned on all sides. Add the garlic, tomato, mushrooms, wine, broth, mixed herbs and bay leaves. Bring to a simmer, cover, and transfer the casserole to the preheated oven for 45–60 minutes, or until everything is tender.

Meanwhile, place the potatoes in a saucepan of boiling water and simmer for 20 minutes, or until just tender. Remove from heat, drain well, and return to the saucepan. Add the milk and mash well. Stir in the Dijon mustard and keep warm.

Using a slotted spoon, remove the meat and vegetables from the casserole and transfer to a warmed serving dish. Cook the sauce on the stove over high heat until reduced by half. Reduce the heat, remove the bay leaves, and adjust the seasoning, adding salt and pepper, if needed.

Mix the cornstarch to a paste with a little cold water. Add to the sauce, stirring well, and bring back to a simmer. Pour the sauce over the meat and vegetables and serve immediately with the mashed potatoes.

Pork with Lemon & Herbs

serves 4

4 tablespoons freshly squeezed orange juice

4 tablespoons red wine vinegar

2 garlic cloves, finely chopped

4 pork steaks, trimmed of all visible fat

Olive oil, for brushing

Freshly ground black pepper

Topping

3 tablespoons finely chopped fresh parsley

Grated rind of 1 lime

Grated rind of ½ lemon

1 garlic clove, very finely chopped

Mix the orange juice, vinegar, and garlic together in a shallow nonmetallic dish and season with pepper to taste. Add the pork, turning to coat. Cover and let marinate in the refrigerator for up to 3 hours.

Meanwhile, mix all the topping ingredients together in a small mixing bowl, cover with plastic wrap, and let chill in the refrigerator until required.

Heat a nonstick ridged grill pan and brush lightly with olive oil. Remove the pork from the marinade, reserving the marinade, add to the pan and cook over medium–high heat for 5 minutes on each side, or until the juices run clear when the meat is pierced with the tip of a sharp knife.

Meanwhile, pour the marinade into a small pan and let simmer over medium heat for 5 minutes, or until slightly thickened. Transfer the pork to a serving dish, pour over the orange sauce, and sprinkle with the gremolata. Serve immediately.

Cinnamon Lamb Casserole

serves 6

2 tablespoons all-purpose flour

2 pound 4 ounces lean boneless lamb, cubed

2 tablespoon olive oil

2 large onions, sliced

1 garlic clove, finely chopped

1¼ cups red wine

2 tablespoons red wine vinegar

One 14.5-ounce can chopped tomatoes

⅓ cup seedless raisins

1 tablespoon ground cinnamon

Pinch of sugar

1 bay leaf

Salt and pepper

Paprika, to garnish

Topping

⅔ cup plain yogurt

2 garlic cloves, crushed

salt and pepper

Season the flour with salt and pepper to taste and put it with the lamb in a plastic bag, then hold the top closed and shake until the lamb cubes are lightly coated all over. Remove the lamb from the bag, then shake off any excess flour and set aside.

Heat the oil in a large, flameproof casserole dish and cook the onions and garlic, stirring frequently, for 5 minutes, or until softened. Add the lamb and cook over high heat, stirring frequently, for 5 minutes, or until browned on all sides and seared.

Stir the wine, vinegar, and tomatoes and their juice into the casserole, scraping any sediment from the bottom of the casserole, and bring to a boil. Reduce the heat and add the raisins, cinnamon, sugar, and bay leaf. Season to taste with salt and pepper. Cover and simmer gently for 2 hours, or until the lamb is tender.

Meanwhile, make the topping. Put the yogurt into a small serving bowl, then stir in the garlic and season to taste with salt and pepper. Cover and chill in the refrigerator until ready to serve.

Discard the bay leaf and serve the lamb hot, topped with a spoonful of the garlic yogurt, and dusted with paprika.

Pork Chops with Sage

2 tablespoons flour

1 tablespoon chopped fresh sage or dried sage

4 lean boneless pork chops, trimmed of excess fat

2 tablespoons olive oil

1 tablespoon butter

2 red onions, sliced into rings

1 tablespoon lemon juice

2 teaspoons sugar

4 plum tomatoes, cut into quarters

Pinch of salt

Freshly ground black pepper

Mix the flour, sage, and salt and pepper to taste on a plate. Lightly dust the pork chops on both sides with the seasoned flour.

Heat the oil and butter in a skillet, add the chops, and cook for 6–7 minutes on each side until cooked through. Drain the chops, reserving the skillet juices, and keep warm.

Toss the onions in the lemon juice and fry along with the sugar and tomatoes for 5 minutes until tender.

Serve the pork with the tomato and onion mixture.

Seven-spice Beef

serves 4

8 ounces long-grain white rice

2½ cups water

12 ounces beef tenderloin, cut into strips

2 tablespoons dark soy sauce

2 tablespoons tomato ketchup

1 tablespoon seven-spice powder

2 tablespoons peanut oil

1 onion, diced

3 small carrots, diced

1 cup frozen peas

2 eggs, beaten

2 tablespoons cold water

Rinse the rice under cold running water, then drain thoroughly. Place the rice in a pan with the water, bring to a boil, cover, and let simmer for 12 minutes. Turn the cooked rice out onto a cookie sheet and let cool.

Using a sharp knife, thinly slice the beef and place in a large, shallow dish.

Mix the soy sauce, tomato ketchup, and seven-spice powder. Spoon over the beef and toss well to coat.

Heat the peanut oil in a preheated wok. Add the beef and stir-fry for 3–4 minutes.

Add the onion, carrots, and peas to the wok and stir-fry for an additional 2–3 minutes. Add the cooked rice to the wok and stir.

Beat the eggs with 2 tablespoons of cold water. Drizzle the egg mixture over the rice and stir-fry for 3–4 minutes, or until the rice is heated through and the egg has set. Transfer the rice and beef to a warmed serving bowl and serve immediately.

Pork with Apples & Berries

serves 4

.1 pound 2 ounce piece lean pork tenderloin

2 teaspoons vegetable oil

⅔ cup fresh vegetable stock

⅔ cup dry rosé wine

1 tablespoon chopped fresh thyme

1 tablespoon clear honey

2 green-skinned apples, cored and sliced, and tossed in 1 tbsp lemon juice

1½ cups prepared fresh or frozen blackberries,

2 teaspoons cornstarch mixed with 4 teaspoons cold water

Pinch of salt

Freshly ground black pepper

Trim away any fat and silvery skin from the pork and cut into ½-inch slices, taking care to keep the slices a good shape.

Heat the oil in a nonstick skillet, add the pork slices, and fry for 4–5 minutes until browned all over. Using a slotted spoon, transfer the pork to paper towels. Reserve the skillet juices.

Pour the stock and wine into the skillet with the juices and add the thyme and honey. Mix well, bring to a simmer, and add the pork and apples. Continue to simmer, uncovered, for 5 minutes.

Add the blackberries, season to taste, and simmer for an additional 5 minutes.

Stir in the cornstarch mixture until thickened.

Pan-fried Lamb

1 tablespoon
vegetable oil

1 tablespoon butter

1 pound 5 ounces lamb
(shoulder or leg), cut
into 1-inch chunks

4 garlic cloves, peeled

3 sprigs of fresh thyme,
stalks removed

6 anchovy fillets

½ cup red wine

½ cup lamb or
vegetable stock

1 teaspoon sugar

1½ cups black olives,
pitted and halved

Heat the oil and butter in a large skillet. Add the lamb and
cook for 4–5 minutes, stirring, until the meat is browned
all over.

Using a pestle and mortar, grind together the garlic, thyme,
and anchovies to make a smooth paste.

Add the wine and stock to the skillet. Stir in the garlic and
anchovy paste together with the sugar.

Bring the mixture to a boil, reduce the heat, cover and
simmer for 30–40 minutes or until the lamb is tender. For
the last 10 minutes of the cooking time, remove the lid to
allow the sauce to reduce slightly.

Stir the olives into the sauce and mix to combine, Warm
thoroughly before serving.

Pork, Sausage & Rice Casserole

2 tablespoons vegetable oil

2 tablespoons butter

1 pound pork tenderloin, cut into thin strips

1 large onion, chopped

1 red bell pepper, seeded and sliced

1 orange bell pepper, seeded and sliced

1 cup sliced mushrooms

¾ cup long-grain rice

1¾ cups beef stock

8 ounces smoked sausage, sliced

¼ teaspoon ground allspice

Salt and freshly ground pepper, to taste

2 tablespoons chopped fresh parsley, to garnish

Preheat the oven to 350°F.

Heat the oil and butter in a large, ovenproof casserole dish. Add the pork and cook over medium heat, stirring, for 5 minutes, until browned. Transfer to a plate.

Add the onion and cook over low heat, stirring occasionally, for 5 minutes, or until softened. Stir in the bell peppers and cook, stirring frequently, for an additional 4–5 minutes. Add the mushrooms and cook for 1 minute, then stir in the rice. Cook for 1 minute, or until the grains are well coated, then add the stock and bring to a boil.

Return the pork to the casserole, add the sausage and allspice, and season to taste with salt and pepper. Mix thoroughly, cover, and cook in the preheated oven for 1 hour, or until all the liquid has been absorbed and the meat is tender. Serve immediately, garnished with chopped parsley.

Pot Roast Pork

serves 4

1 tablespoon
vegetable oil

4 tablespoons (½ stick)
butter

2¼ pound boned and
rolled pork loin

4 shallots, chopped

6 juniper berries
(optional)

2 fresh thyme sprigs,
plus extra to garnish

⅔ cup cider

⅔ cup chicken broth
or water

Salt and freshly ground
pepper, to taste

8 celery ribs, chopped

2 tablespoons all-
purpose flour

⅔ cup heavy cream

Freshly cooked peas,
to serve

Heat the oil with 2 tablespoons of the butter in a heavy
bottom pan or ovenproof casserole dish. Add the pork and
cook over medium heat, turning frequently, for 5–10
minutes, or until browned. Transfer to a plate.

Add the shallots to the pan and cook, stirring frequently, for
5 minutes, or until softened. Add the juniper berries and
thyme sprigs and return the pork to the pan, with any juices
that have collected on the plate. Pour in the cider and
broth, season to taste with salt and pepper, then cover and
simmer for 30 minutes. Turn the pork over and add the
celery. Re-cover the pan and cook for an additional
40 minutes.

Meanwhile, make a paste by mashing the remaining
2 tablespoons of butter with the flour in a small bowl.
Transfer the pork and celery to a platter with a slotted
spoon and keep warm. Remove and discard the juniper
berries and thyme. Whisk the paste, a little at a time, into
the simmering cooking liquid. Cook, stirring constantly, for
2 minutes, then stir in the cream and bring to a boil.

Slice the pork and spoon a little of the sauce over it.
Garnish with thyme sprigs and serve immediately with the
celery, fresh peas, and the remaining sauce.

Sausage & Bean Casserole

8 Italian sausages

3 tablespoons olive oil

1 large onion, chopped

2 garlic cloves, chopped

1 green bell pepper, seeded and sliced

One 14.5-ounce can chopped tomatoes

2 tablespoons sun-dried tomato paste

One 14.5-ounce can cannellini beans

Mashed potatoes or rice, to serve

Prick the sausages all over with a fork. Heat 2 tablespoons of the oil in a large, heavy-bottom skillet. Add the sausages and cook over low heat, turning frequently, for 10–15 minutes, until evenly browned and cooked through. Remove them from the skillet and keep warm. Drain off the oil and wipe out the skillet with paper towels.

Heat the remaining oil in the skillet. Add the onion, garlic, and bell pepper to the skillet and cook for 5 minutes, stirring occasionally, or until softened.

Add the tomatoes to the skillet and let the mixture simmer for about 5 minutes, stirring occasionally, or until slightly reduced and thickened.

Stir the sun-dried tomato paste, cannellini beans, and Italian sausages into the mixture in the skillet. Cook for 4–5 minutes or until the mixture is piping hot. Add 4–5 tablespoons of water if the mixture becomes too dry during cooking.

Transfer the sausage and bean casserole to serving plates and serve with mashed potatoes.

Pork & White Wine Stew

serves 4

²/₃ cup all-purpose flour

Salt and freshly ground pepper, to taste

3 pounds pork tenderloin, cut into ¼-inch slices

4 tablespoons vegetable oil

2 onions, thinly sliced

2 garlic cloves, finely chopped

One 14.5-ounce can chopped tomatoes

1½ cups dry white wine

1 tablespoon torn fresh basil leaves

2 tablespoons chopped fresh parsley

Fresh oregano sprigs, to garnish

Fresh crusty bread, to serve

Spread the flour on a plate and season with salt and pepper. Coat the pork slices in the flour, shaking off any excess. Heat the oil in a ovenproof casserole dish. Add the pork slices and cook over medium heat, turning occasionally, for 4–5 minutes, or until browned all over. Transfer the pork to a plate with a slotted spoon.

Add the onions to the casserole and cook over low heat, stirring occasionally, for 10 minutes, or until golden brown. Add the garlic and cook for an additional 2 minutes, then add the tomatoes, wine, and basil, and season to taste with salt and pepper. Cook, stirring frequently, for 3 minutes.

Return the pork to the casserole, cover, and simmer gently for 1 hour, or until the meat is tender. Add the parsley, garnish with oregano sprigs, and serve immediately with fresh crusty bread.

Hearty Beef Stew

serves 6

3 pounds boneless chuck roast, cut into 2-inch pieces

2 tablespoons vegetable oil

1 teaspoon salt, plus more as needed

Freshly ground black pepper

2 yellow onions, cut into 1-inch pieces

3 tablespoons flour

3 cloves garlic, minced

4 cups cold beef stock or broth

3 carrots, peeled, cut into 1-inch pieces

2 ribs celery, cut into 1-inch pieces

1 tablespoon ketchup

1 bay leaf

¼ teaspoon dried rosemary

¼ teaspoon dried thyme

6 medium Yukon gold potatoes, peeled, cut into large chunks

Fresh parsley to garnish, optional

Season the beef very generously with salt and freshly ground black pepper. Add vegetable oil to a large heavy pot or Dutch oven (one that has a tight fitting lid), and set over high heat. When the oil begins to smoke slightly, add the beef and brown very well. Work in batches if necessary. Once well-browned, remove the beef to a bowl with a slotted spoon, leaving the oil and beef drippings in the pot.

Lower the heat to medium, and add the onions to the pot; sauté about 5 minutes, or until translucent. Add the flour and cook for 2 minutes, stirring often. Add the garlic and cook for 1 minute. Whisk in 1 cup of the beef stock to deglaze the bottom of the pot, scraping up any browned bits caramelized on the bottom. Add the rest of the broth, carrots, celery, ketchup, bay leaf, thyme, rosemary, beef, and 1 teaspoon of salt.

Bring back to a gentle simmer, cover, and cook on low for 1 hour. Add potatoes, and simmer covered for another 30 minutes. Remove the cover, turn up the heat to medium, and cook, stirring occasionally, for another 30 minutes, or until the meat and vegetables are tender.

This last 30 minutes uncovered is not only to finish the cooking, but also to reduce and thicken the sauce. If the stew gets too thick, adjust with some more stock or water. Turn off heat, taste and adjust seasoning, and let sit for 15 minutes before serving. Garnish with fresh parsley, if desired.

Firehouse Chili Con Carne

serves 6

1 tablespoon vegetable oil

1 large yellow onion, diced

2½ pounds lean ground beef

3 cloves garlic, minced

¼ cup chile powder

1 tablespoon ground cumin

1 teaspoon freshly ground black pepper

½ teaspoon chipotle pepper

¼ teaspoon cayenne pepper

1 teaspoon dried oregano

1 teaspoon sugar

1 large green bell pepper, seeded and diced

1 large red bell pepper, seeded and diced

One 15-ounce can tomato sauce

2 tablespoons tomato paste

3 cups water, or more as needed

One 15-ounce can pinto beans, drained, not rinsed

One 15-ounce can kidney beans, drained, not rinsed

Optional Garnishes
Sour cream, grated pepper jack cheese, diced onions, and fresh cilantro leaves

Add the vegetable oil and onions to a Dutch oven, or other heavy pot. Place over medium-high heat and sauté for about 5 minutes, or until the onions begin to soften. Add the ground beef, and cook for about 10 minutes. As the beef browns, use a wooden spoon to break the meat into very small pieces.

Add the garlic, chili powder, ground cumin, black pepper, chipotle pepper, cayenne pepper, oregano, and sugar. Cook, stirring, for 2 minutes.

Stir in the bell peppers, tomato sauce, tomato paste, and water. Bring up to a simmer; reduce the heat to medium-low and cook, uncovered, stirring occasionally for 60 minutes.

After 60 minutes, stir in the beans and simmer for another 30 minutes. If needed, add more water anytime during the cooking to adjust desired thickness. Taste for salt and pepper, and adjust. Serve hot, garnished with sour cream, grated pepper jack, and fresh cilantro leaves, as desired.

Pot-Roasted Leg of Lamb

One 3-4 pound leg of lamb

Salt and freshly ground pepper, to taste

3–4 sprigs of fresh rosemary

4 bacon slices

4 tablespoons olive oil

2–3 garlic cloves, crushed

2 onions, sliced

2 carrots, sliced

2 celery ribs, sliced

1¼ cups dry white wine

1 tablespoon tomato paste

1¼ cups lamb or beef stock

2-3 tomatoes, peeled, cut into quarters, and seeded

1 tablespoon chopped fresh parsley

1 tablespoon chopped fresh oregano or marjoram

Sprigs of fresh rosemary, for garnish

Preheat oven to 350°F.

Wipe the joint of lamb all over, trimming off any excess fat, then season with salt and pepper, rubbing in well. Lay the sprigs of rosemary over the lamb, cover evenly with the bacon slices, and tie in place with string.

Heat the oil in a large skillet and fry the lamb for about 10 minutes, turning several times. Remove the lamb from the skillet, and set aside.

Transfer the oil from the skillet to a large ovenproof casserole and cook the garlic and onion for 3–4 minutes until they begin to soften. Add the carrots and celery and cook for a few minutes longer.

Lay the lamb on top of the vegetables and press down to partly submerge the meat. Pour the wine over the lamb, add the tomato paste, and let simmer for about 3–4 minutes. Add the stock, tomatoes, and herbs and season with salt and pepper to taste. Bring back to a boil for an additional 3–4 minutes.

Cover the casserole tightly and cook in a moderate oven for 2–2½ hours until the lamb is very tender.

Remove the lamb from the casserole and, if preferred, take off the bacon and herbs along with the string. Keep warm. Strain the juices, skimming off any excess fat, and serve in a pitcher. Arrange the vegetables around the lamb, or serve them in a separate dish. Garnish the lamb with the sprigs of rosemary.

Spicy Beef Cobbler

serves 4

2 tablespoons all-purpose flour

Salt and freshly ground pepper, to taste

2 pounds braising beef (chuck or round), cut into bite-size chunks

2 tablespoons olive oil

1 large onion, sliced

1 garlic clove, crushed

1 small fresh red chile, seeded and chopped

1 zucchini, peeled and sliced

1 red bell pepper, seeded and cut into small chunks

1²/₃ cups sliced mushrooms

1 tablespoon tomato paste

2 cups red wine

1 cup beef or vegetable stock

1 bay leaf

Topping

1¼ cups all-purpose flour, plus extra for dusting

2 tablespoons baking powder

Pinch of cayenne pepper

Pinch of salt

3 tablespoons butter

4–5 tablespoons milk

Preheat the oven to 325°F.

Put the flour in a bowl and season well with salt and pepper. Add the beef, toss until well coated, and reserve any remaining seasoned flour. Heat 1 tablespoon of the oil in a large, ovenproof casserole dish. Add the beef and cook, stirring, until browned all over. Remove with a slotted spoon. Heat the remaining tablespoon of the oil in the casserole, add the onion, and garlic, and cook over medium heat, stirring, for 2 minutes, until softened. Add the chile, zucchini, bell pepper, and mushrooms, and cook, stirring, for an additional 3 minutes.

Stir in the reserved seasoned flour and the tomato paste, then stir in the wine. Pour in the stock, add the bay leaf, then bring to a boil. Reduce the heat and cook over low heat, stirring, until thickened. Return the beef to the casserole, cover, and bake in the preheated oven for 45 minutes.

Meanwhile, to make the cobbler topping, sift the flour, baking powder, cayenne pepper, and salt into a mixing bowl. Rub in the butter until the mixture resembles fine breadcrumbs, then stir in enough of the milk to make a smooth dough. Transfer to a lightly floured surface, knead lightly, then roll out to a thickness of about 1/2 inch. Cut out circles using a 2-inch cookie cutter.

Remove the casserole from the oven and discard the bay leaf. Arrange the dough circles over the top, then return to the oven for an additional 30 minutes, or until the topping is golden brown. Serve immediately.

Slow-roasted Pulled Pork with Kansas City Barbeque Sauce

serves 4

3½ to 4 pounds pork shoulder roast

1 teaspoon liquid smoke, optional

For The Dry Rub

2 tablespoons brown sugar

1 tablespoon salt

1 tablespoon freshly ground black pepper

1 tablespoon paprika

2 teaspoons chile powder

2 teaspoons garlic powder

2 teaspoons onion powder

2 teaspoons ground cumin

1 teaspoon cayenne pepper

For The Sauce

2 cups ketchup

⅔ cup dark molasses

½ cup white vinegar

1 teaspoon paprika

1 teaspoon chili powder

1 teaspoon hot sauce

½ teaspoon freshly ground black pepper

½ teaspoon salt

½ teaspoon ground cinnamon

½ teaspoon ground allspice

½ teaspoon ground mace

½ teaspoon liquid smoke, optional

Preheat oven to 215°F. Rinse the meat, and pat dry with paper towels. Trim off any large pieces of excess fat. Mix the rub ingredients together, and thoroughly coat all sides of the pork.

Place the pork, fattier side up, in a large Dutch oven. Pour ⅓ cup water into a small, ovenproof ramekin, and add the liquid smoke, place in the Dutch oven next to the meat. As the pork roasts, this will add moisture as well as a subtle smokiness to the meat. Cover tightly with the lid, and place in the center of the preheated oven. Roast for 12 hours, or until fork tender, or the internal temperature reaches 200°F. Turn off the oven and allow the pork to rest for 1 hour.

To serve, place the pork on a cutting board and using two forks, pull it apart into small pieces. (Some use a knife to chop the succulent meat, but legally you can no longer call it "pulled" pork.) Adjust the seasoning, and serve with the sauce.

For the sauce: Whisk together the ingredients in a saucepan. Bring to a simmer over medium-low heat. Cook, stirring, for 3 minutes. Remove from heat, and let cool to room temperature before serving.

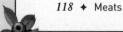

Beef & Vegetable Stew with Corn

serves 4

1 pound braising beef, such as chuck or round

1½ tablespoons all-purpose flour

1 teaspoon hot paprika

1–1½ teaspoons chili powder

1 teaspoon ground ginger

2 tablespoons olive oil

1 large onion, cut into chunks

3 garlic cloves, sliced

2 celery ribs, sliced

4 carrots, chopped

1¼ cups lager

1¼ cups beef stock

2-3 potatoes, chopped

1 red bell pepper, seeded and chopped

2 corn cobs, halved

2 tomatoes, cut into quarters

1 cup shelled fresh or frozen peas

Salt and freshly ground pepper, to taste

1 tablespoon chopped fresh cilantro

Trim any fat or gristle from the beef and cut into 1-inch chunks. Mix the flour and spices together. Toss the beef in the spiced flour until well coated.

Heat the oil in a large, heavy-bottom pan and cook the onion, garlic, and celery, stirring frequently, for 5 minutes, or until softened. Add the beef and cook over high heat, stirring frequently, for 5-8 minutes, or until the meat is browned on all sides and sealed.

Add the carrots, then remove from the heat. Gradually stir in the lager and stock, then return to the heat and bring to a boil, stirring. Reduce the heat, then cover and simmer, stirring occasionally, for 1½ hours.

Add the potatoes to the pan and simmer for an additional 15 minutes. Add the red bell pepper and corn cobs and simmer for 15 minutes, then add the tomato and peas and simmer for an additional 10 minutes, or until the beef and vegetables are tender. Season to taste with salt and pepper, then stir in the cilantro and serve.

Pork Casserole

⅔ cup all-purpose flour

Salt and freshly ground pepper, to taste

3 pounds pork tenderloin, cut into ¼-inch slices

4 tablespoons sunflower oil

2 onions, thinly sliced

2 garlic cloves, finely chopped

One 14.5-ounce can chopped tomatoes in juice

1½ cups dry white wine

1 tablespoon torn fresh basil leaves

2 tablespoons chopped fresh parsley, plus extra sprigs to garnish

Fresh crusty bread, to serve

Spread the flour out on a plate and season to taste with salt and pepper. Toss the pork slices in the flour to coat, shaking off any excess. Heat the oil in a large Dutch oven or ovenproof casserole dish over medium heat. Add the pork slices and cook until browned all over. Using a slotted spoon, transfer the pork to a plate, and reserve.

Add the onions to the casserole dish and cook over low heat, stirring occasionally, for 10 minutes, or until golden brown. Add the garlic and cook, stirring, for 2 minutes, then add the tomatoes with their juice, the wine, and basil leaves, and season to taste with salt and pepper. Cook, stirring frequently, for 3 minutes.

Return the pork to the casserole, cover, and simmer gently for 1 hour, or until the meat is tender. Stir in the chopped parsley. Serve immediately, garnished with parsley sprigs and accompanied by fresh crusty bread.

Irish Stew

serves 4

4 tablespoons all-purpose flour

Salt and freshly ground pepper, to taste

3 pounds lamb shoulder or neck, trimmed of visible fat and cut into 1-inch chunks

3 large onions, chopped

3 carrots, sliced

3 large potatoes, cut into quarters

½ teaspoon dried thyme

3½ cups hot beef stock

2 tablespoons chopped fresh parsley, to garnish

Preheat the oven to 325°F.

Spread the flour on a plate and season with salt and pepper. Roll the pieces of lamb in the flour to coat, shaking off any excess, and arrange in the bottom of a large, ovenproof casserole.

Layer the onions, carrots, and potatoes on top of the lamb. Sprinkle in the thyme and pour in the stock, then cover and cook in the preheated oven for 2½ hours. Add water or more stock if the stew becomes dry.

Garnish with the chopped parsley, and serve straight from the casserole.

Pork with Red Cabbage

serves 4

1 tablespoon vegetable oil

1¾ pound pork loin, boned and rolled

1 onion, finely chopped

1 small red cabbage, thick stems removed and leaves shredded

2 large cooking apples, peeled, cored, and sliced

3 cloves

1 teaspoon brown sugar

3 tablespoons lemon juice, and a thinly pared strip of lemon rind

Lemon wedges, to garnish

Preheat the oven to 325°F.

Heat the oil in a large ovenproof casserole dish. Add the pork and cook over medium heat, turning frequently, for 5–10 minutes, until browned. Transfer to a plate.

Add the chopped onion to the casserole and cook over low heat, stirring occasionally, for 5 minutes, or until softened. Add the cabbage, in batches, and cook, stirring, for 2 minutes. Transfer each batch (mixed with some onion) into a large bowl with a slotted spoon.

Add the apple slices, cloves, and sugar to the bowl and mix well, then place about half the mixture in the bottom of the casserole. Top with the pork and add the remaining cabbage mixture. Sprinkle in the lemon juice and add the strip of rind. Cover and cook in the preheated oven for 1½ hours.

Transfer the pork to a plate. Transfer the cabbage mixture to the plate with a slotted spoon and keep warm. Bring the cooking juices to a boil over high heat and reduce slightly. Slice the pork and arrange on warmed serving plates, surrounded with the cabbage mixture. Spoon the cooking juices over the meat and serve with wedges of lemon.

Yankee Pot Roast

One 5-pound "7-bone" beef chuck roast, or any large chuck roast

Salt and freshly ground black pepper to taste

2 tablespoons vegetable oil

1 tablespoon butter

1 onion, diced

2 ribs celery, chopped

2 tablespoons flour

3 cloves garlic, minced

½ cup red wine

2 teaspoons tomato paste

2 cups chicken broth

1 bay leaf

1 teaspoon dried thyme

½ teaspoon salt

10-12 small new potatoes

4 carrots, peeled, cut in large chunks

2 large parsnips, peeled, cut into chunks

1 tablespoon melted butter

2 tablespoons fresh chopped parsley

Preheat oven to 425°F. Season the beef with salt and pepper. Place a Dutch oven on a high heat on the stove, add the vegetable oil. When the oil is hot, brown the beef, about 5 minutes per side. Remove the meat to a platter, and turn the heat down to medium.

Add the butter, onions, celery, and a pinch of salt. Sauté for 4 to 5 minutes, then add the flour. Cook, stirring, 2 minutes; add the garlic, cook for 1 minute. Whisk in the wine, scraping to deglaze the browned bits from the bottom of the pot. Add the tomato paste, bring to boil, and pour in the chicken broth.

Add the bay leaf, thyme, and salt. Bring the liquid to a simmer, and place the beef back into the pot. Turn the heat to low, and simmer gently for about 45 minutes per pound, or until fork tender. After 2 hours, carefully turn the beef over.

To prepare the vegetables: Add the potatoes, carrots, and parsnips to a shallow roasting pan. Drizzle fat from the beef's braising liquid over the vegetables, along with the melted butter. Toss the vegetables to coat, and season with salt and pepper. Roast in the oven for 20 minutes. Remove and reserve.

About 30 minutes before the beef is done, add the vegetables to the pot. Continue cooking until the beef and vegetables are tender. Taste and adjust for salt and pepper. Remove the beef to a platter. Cut into thick slices or simply tear into large chucks, and serve with the vegetables and gravy. Top with fresh parsley.

Pork Stroganoff

serves 4

12 ounces lean pork fillet

1 tablespoon vegetable oil

1 medium onion, chopped

2 garlic cloves, crushed

2 tablespoons all-purpose flour

2 tablespoons tomato paste

1¾ cups chicken or vegetable stock

1 cup mushrooms, sliced

1 large green bell pepper, cored, seeded, and chopped

½ teaspoon freshly grated nutmeg, plus extra to garnish

4 tablespoons lowfat plain yogurt

Salt and freshly ground pepper, to taste

Cooked rice with chopped fresh parsley, to serve

Trim away any excess fat and silver skin from the pork, then cut the meat into ½-inch thick slices. Heat the vegetable oil in a large, heavy-bottom skillet, add the pork, onion, and garlic, and gently cook for 4–5 minutes, or until the meat is lightly browned.

Stir in the flour and tomato paste, then pour in the chicken stock and stir to mix thoroughly. Add the mushrooms, bell pepper, salt and pepper to taste, and nutmeg. Bring to a boil, cover, reduce heat, and simmer for 20 minutes, or until the pork is tender and cooked through.

Remove the skillet from the heat and stir in the yogurt. Transfer the pork to 4 large, warmed serving plates and serve with cooked rice sprinkled with chopped fresh parsley and an extra spoonful of yogurt, garnished with freshly grated nutmeg.

3

Fish & Seafood

Roasted Seafood

1 pound 5 ounces new potatoes, scrubbed and parboiled for 10–15 minutes

3 red onions, cut into wedges

2 zucchini, cut into chunks

8 garlic cloves, peeled but left whole

2 lemons, cut into wedges

4 fresh rosemary sprigs

4 tablespoons olive oil

12 ounces unshelled raw shrimp

2 small raw squid, cut into rings

4 tomatoes, quartered

Preheat the oven to 400°F.

Place the potatoes in a large roasting pan together with the onions, zucchini, garlic, lemons, and rosemary sprigs.

Pour over the oil and toss to coat all the vegetables in it. Roast in the oven for 30 minutes, turning occasionally, until the potatoes are tender.

Once the potatoes are tender, add the shrimp, squid, and tomatoes, tossing to coat them in the oil, and roast for 10 minutes. All the vegetables should be cooked through and slightly charred for full flavor.

Transfer the roasted seafood and vegetables to warmed serving plates and serve hot.

Mediterranean Fish Casserole

serves 6

2 tablespoons olive oil

1 red onion, peeled and sliced

2 garlic cloves, peeled and chopped

2 red bell peppers, seeded and thinly sliced

One 14.5-ounce can chopped tomatoes

1 teaspoon chopped fresh oregano or marjoram

A few saffron threads soaked in 1 tablespoon warm water for 2 minutes

1 pound white fish (cod, halibut or bass), skinned and boned

1 pound calamari, cut into rings

1¼ cups fish or vegetable stock

8 ounces shelled cooked shrimp plus 6 whole shrimp in their shells

Salt and freshly ground pepper, to taste

2 tablespoons chopped fresh parsley to garnish

Crusty Italian or French bread, to serve

Preheat the oven to 400°F.

Heat the oil in a skillet and cook the onion and garlic over medium heat for 2–3 minutes, or until they begin to soften.

Add the bell peppers to the skillet; continue to cook over low heat for 5 minutes more. Add the tomatoes with the oregano and saffron and stir well.

Cut the white fish into 1¼-inch pieces and place in a Dutch oven or an ovenproof casserole dish. Add the calamari. Pour in the cooked vegetable mixture and the stock, stir well, and season to taste with salt and pepper.

Cover and cook in the center of the preheated oven for 30 minutes or until the fish is tender and cooked. Add the shrimp and just heat through, 2-3 minutes.

Serve the stew hot in bowls garnished with the whole shrimp and the parsley, and with crusty bread to mop up the sauce.

Fried Rice with Shrimp

12 ounces long-grain rice

2 eggs

4 teaspoons cold water

Pinch of salt

Freshly ground black pepper

3 tablespoons vegetable oil

4 scallions, thinly sliced diagonally

1 garlic clove, crushed

1 cup mushrooms, thinly sliced

2 tablespoons oyster or anchovy sauce

One 7-ounce can water chestnuts, drained and sliced

10 ounces shelled shrimp, thawed, if frozen

½ bunch watercress, roughly chopped

Sprigs of watercress, for garnish (optional)

Place the rice in a pan with 2–3 cups lightly salted water, bring to a boil, cover, and let simmer for 12 minutes. Set aside and keep warm.

Beat each egg separately with 2 teaspoons of cold water and salt and pepper.

Heat 2 teaspoons of the oil in a wok or large skillet, swirling it around until really hot. Pour in the first egg, swirl it around, and let cook undisturbed until set. Remove to a plate or board and repeat with the second egg. Cut the omelets into 1-inch squares.

Heat the remaining oil in the wok and, when really hot, add the scallions and garlic and stir-fry for 1 minute. Add the mushrooms and continue to cook for an additional 2 minutes.

Stir in the oyster sauce and seasoning and add the water chestnuts and shrimp; stir-fry for 2 minutes.

Stir in the cooked rice and stir-fry for 1 minute, then add the watercress and omelet squares and stir-fry for an additional 1–2 minutes until piping hot. Serve at once, garnished with the sprigs of watercress, if using.

Shrimp in Green Sauce

serves 4

2 tablespoons vegetable oil

3 onions, chopped

5 garlic cloves, chopped

5–7 ripe tomatoes, diced

1½ cups green beans, cut into 2-inch pieces and blanched for 1 minute

¼ teaspoon ground cumin

Pinch of ground allspice

Pinch of ground cinnamon

1 canned chipotle chile in marinade, with some of the marinade

2 cups fish stock or water mixed with a fish bouillon cube

1 pound raw shrimp, shelled

Sprigs of fresh cilantro, for garnish

1 lime, cut into wedges

Heat the oil in a large pan. Add the onions and garlic and cook over low heat, stirring occasionally, for about 5–10 minutes until softened. Add the tomatoes and cook for 2 minutes.

Add the green beans, cumin, allspice, cinnamon, chipotle chile and marinade, and stock. Bring to a boil, then reduce the heat, and simmer for a few minutes to combine the flavors.

Add the shrimp and cook, stirring gently, for 1–2 minutes only, then remove the pan from the heat and set the shrimp aside to steep in the hot liquid to finish cooking. They are cooked when they have turned a bright pink color.

Serve the shrimp immediately, garnished with the cilantro and accompanied by the lime wedges.

Fishermans Pie

serves 6

2 pounds white fish fillets (cod, halibut or bass), skinned

Salt and freshly ground pepper, to taste

²⁄₃ cup dry white wine

1 tablespoon chopped fresh parsley, tarragon, or dill

½ cup (1 stick) butter, plus extra for greasing

1 cup sliced mushrooms

8 ounces cooked, peeled shrimp

2 tablespoons all-purpose flour

½ cup heavy cream

2 pounds (about 6) Idaho potatoes, peeled and cut into chunks

Preheat the oven to 350°F. Grease a 7½-cup casserole dish.

Fold the fish fillets in half and put in the prepared dish. Season well with salt and pepper, pour over the wine, and scatter over the parsley. Cover with foil and bake in the preheated oven for 15 minutes, until the fish starts to flake. Strain off the liquid and reserve for the sauce. Increase the oven temperature to 425°F.

Melt 1 tablespoon of the butter in a skillet over medium heat, add the mushrooms, and cook, stirring frequently, for 5 minutes. Spoon over the fish, then scatter the shrimp over the mushrooms.

Heat 4 tablespoons of the remaining butter in a pan and stir in the flour. Cook for 3–4 minutes, without browning, stirring constantly. Remove from the heat and gradually add the reserved cooking liquid, stirring well after each addition. Return to the heat and slowly bring to a boil, stirring constantly, until thickened. Add the cream and season to taste with salt and pepper. Pour over the fish in the dish and smooth over the surface.

Bring a large pan of lightly salted water to a boil, add the potatoes, and cook for 15–20 minutes. Drain well and mash until smooth. Season to taste with salt and pepper, then add the remaining butter, stirring until melted. Pile or pipe the potato onto the fish and sauce and bake for 10–15 minutes, until golden brown. Serve immediately.

Moroccan Fish Stew

serves 4

2 tablespoons olive oil

1 large onion, finely chopped

Pinch of saffron threads

½ teaspoon ground cinnamon

1 teaspoon ground coriander

½ teaspoon ground cumin

½ teaspoon ground turmeric

1 cup canned chopped tomatoes

1¼ cups fish stock

4 small red snappers, cleaned, boned, and heads and tails removed

¼ cup green olives

1 tablespoon chopped preserved lemon

3 tablespoons chopped fresh cilantro

Salt and pepper

Heat the olive oil in a Dutch oven or ovenproof casserole dish. Add the onion and cook gently over very low heat, stirring occasionally, for 10 minutes, or until softened, but not colored. Add the saffron, cinnamon, ground coriander, cumin, and turmeric, and cook for an additional 30 seconds, stirring constantly.

Add the tomatoes and fish stock and stir well. Bring to a boil, reduce the heat, cover, and simmer for 15 minutes. Uncover and simmer for 20–35 minutes, or until the sauces has thickened.

Cut each red snapper in half, then add the fish pieces to the casserole, pushing them down into the liquid. Simmer the stew for an additional 5–6 minutes, or until the fish is just cooked.

Carefully stir in the olives, preserved lemon, and fresh cilantro. Season to taste with salt and pepper, and serve immediately.

Clams Casino

makes 18

18 medium-sized (about 2½ inches) of littleneck clams

2 tablespoons unsalted butter

3 strips center-cut bacon, each sliced into 6 equal pieces (18 total)

3 tablespoons finely diced red bell pepper

3 garlic cloves, finely minced

⅓ cup plain breadcrumbs

1 tablespoon finely grated Parmesan

⅛ teaspoon freshly ground black pepper

Pinch of salt

2 tablespoons chopped flat leaf parsley

Lemon wedges

Rock salt as needed

Heat butter in a skillet over medium heat. Add the bacon and sauté until cooked, but not quite crisp. Using a slotted spoon, transfer the bacon to a plate and reserve.

Add the red pepper to the bacon drippings in the skillet, and cook for 2 minutes. Add the garlic and cook for 1 minute more. Turn off the heat and stir in the breadcrumbs, Parmesan, black pepper, and salt. Reserve the mixture until needed.

Add about 2 inches of water to a Dutch oven, or other heavy pot with a tight-fitting lid, and bring to a rapid boil over high heat. Add clams, cover, and cook for about 5 minutes, or just until the shells open. It's critical to remove and drain the clams as soon as they open. Allow the clams to cool until they can be handled.

Twist and pull the clamshells apart, and remove the clam. Place the clam back into the deeper of the two shell halves. Spread the rock salt on a heatproof baking dish, and set the clams on top of the salt, pressing in slightly.

Divide the breadcrumb mixture evenly over the top of each clamshell, and top with one piece of bacon. Broil on high, about 8 inches from the heat, until the tops are browned and the edges of the bacon are crisp. Sprinkle on the fresh parsley, and serve hot with lemon wedges.

Drunken Mussels

4 tablespoons butter

4 cloves garlic, sliced thin

1 shallot, thinly sliced

1½ cups white wine

¼ cup chopped fresh Italian parsley

½ tablespoon lemon zest

Pinch of red pepper flakes, optional

3 pounds fresh mussels, scrubbed and rinsed

Lemon wedges, optional

Add the butter to a large stockpot (one with a tight-fitting lid). Melt it over medium heat, and add the garlic and shallots; cook for one minute, or until they begin to sizzle.

Add the wine, parsley, lemon zest, and pepper flakes. Turn the heat to high and bring the mixture to a boil. Add the mussels and cover quickly. Cook for 3 minutes, give the pot a little shake back and forth, and cook for another 2 to 4 minutes, or until the mussels have opened.

As soon as the shells open, serve immediately. The mussels will shrivel up to nothing if left to simmer in the hot liquid. Divide among some deep bowls. Taste the broth for salt (usually the mussels provide enough natural salt, but add some if needed). Ladle some of the broth over each bowl, and dig in. Serve with extra lemon wedges if desired.

Catfish Stew

1 teaspoon garlic powder

1 teaspoon celery salt

1 teaspoon pepper

1 teaspoon curry powder

1 teaspoon paprika

Pinch of sugar

2 pounds catfish or rockfish

2 tablespoons red wine vinegar

2 tablespoons all-purpose flour

6 tablespoons corn oil

1 onion, finely chopped

2 garlic cloves, finely chopped

2 medium tomatoes, peeled and chopped

1 fresh marjoram sprig

2½ cups fish stock

¼ teaspoon ground cumin

¼ teaspoon ground cinnamon

2 fresh red or green chiles, seeded and finely chopped

1 red bell pepper, seeded and finely chopped

1 yellow bell pepper, seeded and finely chopped

Salt, to taste

Fresh Italian parsley sprigs, to garnish

Crusty bread, to serve

Mix together the garlic powder, celery salt, pepper, curry powder, paprika, and sugar in a small bowl.

Place the fish in a nonmetallic dish and sprinkle with half the spice mixture. Turn the fish over and sprinkle with the remaining spice mixture. Add the vinegar and turn to coat. Cover with plastic wrap and set aside in a cool place to marinate for 1 hour.

Spread out the flour in a shallow dish. Drain the fish and dip into the flour to coat, shaking off any excess.

Heat 4 tablespoons of the oil in a skillet. Add the fish and cook over medium heat for 2–3 minutes on each side. Remove with a slotted spoon and set aside.

Wipe out the skillet with paper towels, add the remaining oil, and heat. Add the onion and cook over low heat, stirring occasionally, for 5 minutes, until soft. Add the garlic and cook, stirring, for an additional 2 minutes. Add the tomatoes and marjoram, increase the heat to medium, and cook, stirring occasionally, for 8 minutes.

Stir in the fish stock, cumin, and cinnamon, and add the fish, chiles, and bell peppers. Bring to a boil, then reduce the heat and simmer for 8–10 minutes, until the fish flakes easily and the sauce has thickened. Season to taste with salt.

Garnish with parsley sprigs and serve immediately with warm crusty bread.

Spanish-style Swordfish in Tomato Sauce

serves 4

4 tablespoons lemon juice

6 tablespoons olive oil

Salt and pepper, to taste

4 6-ounce swordfish steaks

1 onion, finely chopped

1 garlic clove, finely chopped

1 tablespoon all-purpose flour

6 tomatoes, peeled, seeded, and chopped

1 tablespoon tomato paste

1¼ cups dry white wine

Fresh dill sprigs, to garnish

To marinate the fish: Place the lemon juice and 4 tablespoons of the olive oil in a shallow, nonmetallic dish, stir well, then season to taste with salt and pepper. Add the swordfish steaks, turning to coat thoroughly, then cover with plastic wrap and let marinate in the refrigerator for 1 hour.

Preheat the oven to 350°F.

Heat the remaining oil in a flameproof casserole dish. Add the onion and cook over low heat, stirring occasionally, for 10 minutes, or until golden. Add the garlic and cook, stirring frequently, for 2 minutes. Sprinkle in the flour and cook, stirring, for 1 minute, then add the tomatoes, tomato paste, and wine. Bring to a boil, stirring.

Add the fish to the casserole, pushing it down into the liquid. Cover and cook in the preheated oven for 20 minutes, or until cooked through and the flesh flakes easily. Serve garnished with dill sprigs.

Maryland Crab Cakes with Tartar Sauce

serves 4

1 large egg, beaten

2 tablespoons mayonnaise

½ teaspoon Dijon mustard

¼ teaspoon Worcestershire sauce

½ teaspoon Old Bay seasoning

¼ teaspoon salt, or to taste

Pinch of cayenne pepper, optional

1 pound fresh lump crabmeat, well drained

10 saltine crackers

Plain breadcrumbs, or as needed

1 tablespoon vegetable oil

2 tablespoons unsalted butter

For The Tartar Sauce

1 cup mayonnaise

¼ cup sweet pickle relish

1 tablespoon finely minced onion

1 tablespoon chopped capers

1 tablespoon chopped parsley

1½ tablespoons freshly squeezed lemon juice

Dash of Worcestershire sauce

Few drops of Tabasco, optional

Salt and freshly ground black pepper to taste

Whisk together the egg, mayonnaise, mustard, Worcestershire, Old Bay, salt, and cayenne to a mixing bowl. Crush the crackers into very fine crumbs and add to the bowl. Stir until combined. Let sit for 5 minutes.

Gently fold in the crabmeat. Cover the bowl and refrigerate for at least 1 hour.

Sprinkle the breadcrumbs lightly over a large plate. Shape the crab mixture into 6 cakes, and place on the plate. Dust the tops of each crab cake lightly with more breadcrumbs. These cakes are almost all crab, which makes them fragile. They will bind together as the egg cooks, and golden-brown crust forms.

Heat the vegetable oil and butter in a large skillet over medium-high heat. When the foam from the butter begins to dissipate, carefully transfer each crab cake to the pan. Sauté until golden brown, about 4 minutes per side. Drain on a paper towel, and serve with the sauce.

For the sauce: Mix together all the ingredients in a bowl. Refrigerate at least an hour before serving. Makes 1½ cups.

New England Clam Chowder

serves 6

1 cup water

1 pound little neck clams, washed

2 slices bacon, cut into ¼ inch pieces

1 tablespoon butter

½ yellow onion, diced

2 tablespoons flour

2 (10 ounce) cans whole clams, drained

2 cups cold clam juice (Part of this may be made up from the drained canned clam liquid, but clam juice has a stronger clam flavor)

1½ pounds (5 medium) Idaho potatoes, peeled, and cut into ¼ inch cubes

1 cup milk

1 cup cream

Salt and freshly ground black pepper to taste

Fresh chopped parsley to garnish

Oyster crackers, to garnish

Bring one cup of water to a boil in a small saucepan over high heat. Add the little neck clams, cover tightly, and cook for a couple minutes, until the clams open. Remove the clams to a bowl and reserve. Strain the cooking liquid and reserve.

In large saucepan, over medium heat, cook the bacon in the butter until almost crisp. Remove the bacon with slotted spoon and reserve, leaving the butter and rendered bacon fat in the pan.

Reduce the heat to medium-low, and add the onions. Sauté until soft and translucent, about 5 minutes. Add the flour and cook, stirring, for 2 minutes. Whisk in the cold clam juice, slowly at first. Add the reserved clam cooking liquid. Bring back to a simmer and add the potatoes. Cover and cook for 20 minutes, or until the potatoes are tender.

Note: At this point some chowder-heads like to smash some of the potatoes against the bottom of the pan with a masher to add body to the soup. Optional!

Stir in the canned clams, milk, and cream. Reduce heat to low, and cook until just heated through. Do not boil. Add the reserved little neck clams, and cook for another minute. Taste and season with salt and freshly ground black pepper as needed.

Serve hot topped with the reserved bacon, parsley, and oyster crackers.

Mussels in White Wine Sauce

serves 4

4 pounds 8 ounces mussels

1¼ cups dry white wine

6 shallots, finely chopped

1 tablespoon mixed herbs

1 bay leaf

Freshly ground black pepper, to taste

4 bay leaves, to garnish

Crusty bread, to serve

Mussels should be closed when purchased; if they are open slightly, they should close quickly if tapped with a knife; discard any with broken shells and any that refuse to close. To clean the mussels, scrub and scrape them thoroughly, and gently pull off any beards. Rinse the mussels under cold running water.

Pour the wine into a large, heavy-bottom pan, add the shallots, bay leaf and mixed herbs and season to taste with pepper. Bring to a boil over medium heat. Add the mussels, cover tightly, and cook, shaking the pan occasionally, for 5 minutes. Remove and discard the bay leaf and any mussels that have not opened.

Divide the mussels among four bowls with a slotted spoon. Tilt the casserole to let any sediment settle, then spoon the cooking liquid over the mussels, garnish each bowl with a bay leaf, and serve immediately with crusty bread.

Shrimp with Coconut Rice

serves 4

1 cup dried Chinese mushrooms

2 tablespoons vegetable oil

6 scallions, trimmed and chopped

½ cup dry unsweetened shredded coconut

1 fresh green chile, seeded and chopped

1 cup jasmine rice

⅔ cup fish stock

1¾ cups coconut milk

12 ounces cooked shelled shrimp

6 sprigs fresh Thai basil

Place the mushrooms in a small bowl, cover with hot water, and set aside to soak for 30 minutes. Drain, then cut off and discard the stalks and slice the caps.

Heat the oil in a wok and stir-fry the scallions, coconut, and chile for 2–3 minutes, until lightly browned. Add the mushrooms and stir-fry for 3–4 minutes.

Add the rice and stir-fry for 2–3 minutes, then add the stock and bring to a boil. Reduce the heat and add the coconut milk.

Let simmer for 10–15 minutes, until the rice is tender. Stir in the shrimp and basil, heat through, and serve.

Spicy Scallops with Lime & Chile

serves 4

16 large scallops

1 tablespoon butter

1 tablespoon vegetable oil

1 teaspoon minced garlic

1 teaspoon fresh ginger, grated

4 scallions, trimmed and sliced thinly

Finely grated peel of 1 lime

1 small fresh red chile, seeded and very finely chopped

3 tablespoons lime juice

Lime wedges, to serve

4 cups cooked rice, to serve

Trim the scallops, then wash, and pat dry. Separate the corals from the white parts, then slice each white part in half horizontally, making 2 circles.

Heat the butter and vegetable oil in a wok or skillet. Add the garlic and ginger and stir-fry for 1 minute without browning. Add the scallions and stir-fry for 1 minute.

Add the scallops and stir-fry over high heat for 4–5 minutes. Stir in the lime peel, chile, and lime juice and cook for 1 minute more.

Serve the scallops hot, with the juices spooned over them, accompanied by lime wedges and cooked rice.

Bouillabaise

8 ounces live mussels

½ cup olive oil

3 garlic cloves, chopped

2 onions, chopped

2 tomatoes, seeded and chopped

2¾ cups fish stock

1¾ cups white wine

1 bay leaf

Pinch of saffron threads

2 tablespoons chopped fresh basil

2 tablespoons chopped fresh parsley

8 ounces snapper or monkfish fillets

8 ounces halibut or swordfish fillets, skinned

8 ounces shrimp, peeled and deveined

4 ounces scallops

Salt and freshly ground pepper, to taste

Fresh French baguettes, to serve

Soak the mussels in lightly salted water for 10 minutes. Scrub the shells under cold running water and pull off any beards. Discard any with broken shells. Tap the remaining mussels and discard any that refuse to close. Put the rest into a large pan with a little water, bring to a boil, and cook over high heat for 4 minutes. Transfer the cooked mussels to a bowl, discarding any that remain closed, and reserve. Wipe out the pan with paper towels.

Heat the oil in the pan over medium heat. Add the garlic and onions and cook, stirring, for 3 minutes. Stir in the tomatoes, stock, wine, bay leaf, saffron, and herbs. Bring to a boil, reduce the heat, cover, and simmer for 30 minutes.

When the tomato mixture is cooked, rinse the fish, pat dry, and cut into chunks. Add to the pan and simmer for 5 minutes. Add the mussels, shrimp, and scallops, and season. Cook for 3 minutes, until the fish is cooked through.

Remove from the heat, discard the bay leaf, and ladle into serving bowls. Serve with fresh French baguettes.

Tuna & Vegetable Stir-fry

serves 4

2 large carrots, cut into sticks

1 onion

2½ cups baby corn

2 tablespoons corn oil

3½ cups snow peas

1 pound fresh tuna

2 tablespoons fish sauce

1 tablespoon palm sugar

Finely grated zest and juice of 1 orange

2 tablespoons sherry

1 teaspoon cornstarch

Rice or noodles, for serving

Using a sharp knife, cut the carrots into thin sticks, slice the onion, and halve the baby corn.

Heat the corn oil in a large preheated wok or skillet.

Add the onion, carrots, snow peas, and baby corn to the wok and stir-fry for 5 minutes.

Using a sharp knife, thinly slice the tuna.

Add the tuna slices to the wok and stir-fry for about 2–3 minutes or until the tuna turns opaque.

Mix together the fish sauce, sugar, orange zest and juice, sherry, and cornstarch.

Pour the mixture over the tuna and vegetables and cook for 2 minutes, or until the juices thicken. Serve the stir-fry with the rice.

Fried Shrimp with Cashews

2 garlic cloves, crushed

1 tablespoon cornstarch

Pinch of sugar

1 pound raw jumbo shrimp

4 tablespoons vegetable oil

1 leek, sliced

1½ cups broccoli florets

1 orange bell pepper, seeded and diced

1 cup unsalted cashews

Sauce

¾ cup fish stock

1 tablespoon cornstarch

dash of chili sauce

2 teaspoons sesame oil

1 tablespoon Chinese rice wine

Mix together the garlic, cornstarch, and sugar in a bowl.

Shell and devein the shrimp. Stir the shrimp into the mixture to coat thoroughly.

Heat the vegetable oil in a preheated wok and add the shrimp mixture. Stir-fry over high heat for 20–30 seconds until the shrimp turn pink. Remove the shrimp from the wok with a slotted spoon, drain on paper towels, and set aside until required.

Add the leek, broccoli, and bell pepper to the wok and stir-fry for 2 minutes.

To make the sauce, place the fish stock, cornstarch, chili sauce to taste, sesame oil, and rice wine in a small bowl. Mix until thoroughly combined.

Add the sauce to the wok, together with the cashews. Return the shrimp to the wok and cook for 1 minute to heat through.

Transfer the shrimp to a warmed serving dish and serve immediately.

Macaroni & Seafood Casserole

serves 4

12 ounces dried macaroni

6 tablespoons (¾ stick) butter, plus extra for greasing

2 small fennel bulbs, trimmed and thinly sliced

2 cups sliced mushrooms

6 ounces cooked, peeled shrimp

Pinch of cayenne pepper

1¼ cups béchamel sauce

½ cup freshly grated Parmesan cheese

2 large tomatoes, sliced

Olive oil, for brushing

1 teaspoon dried oregano

Salt, to taste

Preheat the oven to 350°F. Grease a large, ovenproof casserole dish.

Bring a large saucepan of lightly salted water to a boil. Add the macaroni, return to a boil, and cook for 8–10 minutes, or until tender but still firm to the bite. Drain and return to the pan. Add 2 tablespoons of the butter to the pasta, cover, shake the pan, and keep warm.

Melt 4 tablespoons butter in a separate pan. Add the fennel and cook for 3–4 minutes. Stir in the mushrooms and cook for an additional 2 minutes. Stir in the shrimp, then remove the pan from the heat.

Stir the cooked pasta, cayenne pepper, and the shrimp mixture into the béchamel sauce*. Pour into the prepared dish and spread evenly. Sprinkle the Parmesan over the casserole, and arrange the tomato slices around the edge. Brush the tomatoes with the olive oil, then sprinkle the oregano over the top. Bake in the preheated oven for 25 minutes, or until golden brown. Serve immediately.

To make a bechamel sauce melt 5 tablespoons butter over a medium heat. Add 4 tablespoons of all-purpose flour and stir until smooth. Cook over a medium heat until a light golden color. Add 4 cups of warmed whole milk and bring to the boil whisking thoroughly. Add 1 teaspoon fresh or powdered nutmeg and ½ teaspoon salt.

Seafood Lasagna

serves 4

3 ½ tablespoons butter, plus extra for greasing

5 tablespoons all-purpose flour

1 teaspoon mustard powder

2½ cups whole milk

2 tablespoons olive oil

1 onion, chopped

2 garlic cloves, finely chopped

3 cups mixed mushrooms, sliced

²/₃ cup white wine

One 14.5-ounce can chopped tomatoes

Salt and freshly ground black pepper, to taste

1 pound skinless white fish fillets (cod, halibut or bass)

8 ounces fresh scallops

4–6 sheets fresh lasagna

1 cup mozzarella cheese, shredded

Preheat the oven to 400°F. Lightly grease a lasagna pan or a 9x13-inch cake pan.

Melt the butter in a heavy saucepan over low heat. Add the flour and mustard powder and stir until smooth. Simmer gently for 2 minutes, but do not allow the flour to color or burn. Gradually add the milk, whisking until smooth. Bring the sauce to a boil, reduce the heat, and simmer for 2 minutes. Remove from the heat, cover the surface of the sauce with plastic wrap to prevent a skin forming, and set aside.

Heat the olive oil in a skillet. Add the onion and garlic and cook gently for 5 minutes, or until softened. Add the mushrooms and cook for 5 minutes, or until softened. Stir in the wine and boil rapidly until almost evaporated, then stir in the tomatoes. Bring to a boil, reduce the heat, and simmer, covered, for 15 minutes. Season to taste with salt and pepper, and reserve.

Cut the fish into cubes. Spoon half the tomato mixture into the lasagna pan, top with half the fish and scallops, and layer half the lasagna over the top. Pour half the white sauce over the lasagna, and sprinkle on half the mozzarella cheese. Repeat these layers, finishing with sauce and mozzarella cheese.

Bake the lasagna in the preheated oven for 35–40 minutes, or until the top is golden and the fish is cooked through. Remove from the oven and let stand for 10 minutes before serving.

Southwestern Seafood Stew

serves 4

1 yellow bell pepper,
1 red bell pepper,
1 orange bell pepper,
seeded and cut into quarters

1 pound (about 3) large ripe
tomatoes

2 large, fresh, mild green
chiles, such as poblano

6 garlic cloves, peeled but
kept whole

2 teaspoons dried oregano
or dried mixed herbs

2 tablespoons olive oil, plus
extra for drizzling

1 large onion, finely chopped

2 cups fish, vegetable, or
chicken stock

Finely grated rind and juice
of 1 lime

2 tablespoons chopped fresh
cilantro, plus extra to
garnish

1 bay leaf

1 pound red snapper fillets,
skinned and cut into chunks

8 ounces raw shrimp,
shelled and deveined

8 ounces raw calamari rings

Salt and freshly ground
black pepper, to taste

Warmed flour tortillas,
to serve

Preheat the oven to 400°F.

Put the pepper quarters, skin-side up, in a roasting pan with the tomatoes, chiles, and garlic. Sprinkle with the oregano and drizzle with oil. Roast in the preheated oven for 30 minutes, or until the bell peppers are well browned and softened.

Remove the roasted vegetables from the oven and let stand until cool enough to handle. Peel off the skins from the bell peppers, tomatoes, and chiles and chop the flesh. Finely chop the garlic.

Heat the oil in a large pan and cook the onion, stirring frequently, for 5 minutes, or until softened. Add the bell peppers, tomatoes, chiles, garlic, stock, lime rind and juice, cilantro, bay leaf, and salt and pepper to taste. Bring to a boil, then stir in the fish, shrimp, and calamari.

Reduce the heat, then cover and simmer gently for 10 minutes, or until the fish and calamari are just cooked through and the shrimp have turned pink. Discard the bay leaf, then garnish with chopped cilantro before serving, accompanied by warmed flour tortillas.

Baked Lemon Sole

2 garlic cloves
4 lemon sole fillets
1 shallot, finely chopped
2 tablespoons fresh thyme, plus extra for garnish
Grated rind and juice of 1 lemon
2 tablespoons olive oil
Pinch of salt
Freshly ground black pepper

Preheat the oven to 350°F.

Using a sharp knife, thinly slice the garlic and set aside.

Arrange the sole fillets in a single layer in the bottom of a large ovenproof dish and sprinkle with the shallot.

Place the garlic slices and the thyme on top of the fillets and season with salt and pepper to taste. Mix the lemon juice, rind and olive oil together and pour over the fish.

Bake in the preheated oven for 15 minutes, or until the fish flakes easily when tested with a fork.

Garnish with lemon rind/slices or herbs, and serve immediately.

Noodles with Chile & Shrimp

serves 4

8 ounces thin glass noodles

2 tablespoons vegetable oil

1 onion, sliced

2 red chiles, seeded and very finely chopped

4 lime leaves, thinly shredded

1 tablespoon fresh cilantro

2 tablespoons sugar

2 tablespoons fish sauce

1 pound jumbo shrimp, shelled

Place the noodles in a large bowl. Pour over enough boiling water to cover the noodles and let stand for 5 minutes. Drain thoroughly and set aside until required.

Heat the oil in a large preheated wok or skillet until it is really hot.

Add the onion, chiles, and lime leaves to the wok and stir-fry for 1 minute.

Add the cilantro, sugar, fish sauce, and shrimp to the wok and stir-fry for an additional 2 minutes or until the shrimp turn pink.

Add the drained noodles to the wok, toss to mix well, and stir-fry for 1–2 minutes or until heated through.

Transfer the noodles and shrimp to warmed serving bowls and serve immediately.

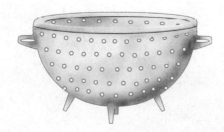

Flounder in Melted Cheese

serves 4

2 tablespoons olive oil, plus extra for brushing

4 6-ounce flounder fillets

Grated rind and juice of 2 lemons

Salt and pepper, to taste

½ cup Swiss cheese, grated

4 tablespoons fresh white bread crumbs

4 tablespoons sour cream

4 garlic cloves, finely chopped

Lemon wedges, to garnish

Fresh parsley sprigs, to garnish

Preheat the oven to 400°F.

Brush a roasting pan or large ovenproof dish with olive oil.

Arrange the fish in a single layer in the roasting pan. Sprinkle with a little lemon juice and season to taste with salt and pepper.

Mix the olive oil, grated cheese, bread crumbs, sour cream, garlic, lemon rind, and 6 tablespoons of the remaining lemon juice together in a large bowl and season to taste with salt and pepper. Spread the cheese paste evenly over the fish fillets.

Bake in the preheated oven for 12–15 minutes, or until the fish is cooked through. Transfer to warmed serving plates, garnish with lemon wedges and parsley sprigs, and serve immediately.

Classic Tuna Noodle Casserole

serves 6

3 tablespoons butter

½ yellow onion, finely diced

3 tablespoons flour

3½ cups cold milk

1 (10.5-ounce) can condensed cream of mushroom soup

1 teaspoon salt

¼ teaspoon freshly ground black pepper

12 ounce package dry egg noodles

2 (5-ounce) cans tuna, well drained, crumbled

¾ cup frozen peas, thawed, drained

1 cup shredded cheddar cheese

½ cup shredded Monterey jack cheese

½ cup plain bread crumbs

2 tablespoons olive oil

Preheat oven to 350°F.

Melt the butter in a medium saucepan, over medium-low heat, and sauté the onions for about 4 minutes, or until translucent. Turn up the heat to medium; add the flour, and cook, stirring, for another 2 minutes. While whisking vigorously, slowly pour in one cup of the cold milk.

When the mixture begins to simmer, add the rest of the milk, can of mushroom soup, salt, and pepper. Cook, stirring occasionally, until the sauce thickens, and comes to a simmer. Remove from heat, and reserve.

Cook noodles in boiling salted water, one minute less than the directions call for. Drain well, and add to a large mixing bowl. Add the sauce, tuna, peas and about two-thirds of the cheese. Mix with a spatula to combine.

Pour the mixture into a lightly oiled 9 x 13-casserole dish, and top with the rest of the cheese. Mix the breadcrumbs and olive oil together in a small bowl until combined. Sprinkle evenly over the casserole. Bake for 35 minutes, or until browned and bubbly.

4

Vegetarian

Root Vegetable & Pumpkin Casserole

serves 4

1 onion, sliced

2 leeks, trimmed, thoroughly washed, and sliced

2 celery ribs, chopped

2 carrots, thinly sliced

1 red bell pepper, seeded and sliced

1¾ cups diced pumpkin

1⅔ cups diced mixed root vegetables, such as sweet potato or parsnip

One 14.5-ounce can chopped tomatoes

1 cup cider (or apple juice)

2 teaspoons dried mixed herbs

Salt and freshly ground pepper

Fresh Italian parsley leaves, to garnish

Preheat the oven to 350°F.

Put the onion, leeks, celery, carrots, bell pepper, pumpkin, and root vegetables in a large casserole dish and mix well.

Stir in the tomatoes, ⅔ cup of the cider (or apple juice) and the dried mixed herbs. Season to taste with salt and pepper.

Cover and bake in the preheated oven, stirring once or twice, and adding a little extra cider, or apple juice if extra liquid is needed, for 1¼ hours, or until the vegetables are cooked through and tender.

Serve immediately, garnished with parsley leaves.

Eggplant Gratin

serves 2

4 tablespoons olive oil

2 onions, finely chopped

2 garlic cloves, very finely chopped

2 eggplants, thickly sliced

3 tablespoons fresh flat-leaf parsley, chopped

½ teaspoon dried thyme

One 14.5-ounce can chopped tomatoes

2 cups coarsely grated mozzarella

6 tablespoons freshly grated Parmesan

Salt and pepper

Preheat the oven to 400°F.

Heat the oil in a flameproof casserole over medium heat. Add the onions and cook for 5 minutes or until soft. Add the garlic and cook for a few seconds or until just beginning to color. Using a slotted spoon, transfer the onion mixture to a plate.

Cook the eggplant slices in batches in the same flameproof casserole dish until they are just lightly browned. Transfer to another plate.

Arrange a layer of eggplant slices in the bottom of the casserole dish. Sprinkle with the parsley, thyme, and salt and pepper. Add a layer of onion, tomatoes, and mozzarella, sprinkling parsley, thyme, and salt and pepper over each layer.

Continue layering, finishing with a layer of eggplant slices. Sprinkle with the Parmesan.

Bake, uncovered, for 20–30 minutes or until the top is golden and the eggplants are tender. Serve hot.

Cold Weather Casserole

serves 6

¼ cup (½ stick) butter

2 leeks, sliced

2 carrots, sliced

2 potatoes, cut into bite-size pieces

½ squash, cut into bite-size pieces

2 zucchini, sliced

1 fennel bulb, halved and sliced

2 tablespoons all-purpose flour

One 15-ounce can lima beans

2½ cups vegetable stock

2 tablespoons tomato paste

1 teaspoon dried thyme

2 bay leaves

Pinch of salt

Freshly ground black pepper

Melt the butter in a large, heavy-bottom pan over low heat. Add the leeks, carrots, potatoes, squash, zucchini, and fennel and cook, stirring occasionally, for 10 minutes.

Stir in the flour and cook, stirring continuously, for 1 minute. Stir in the can juice from the beans, the stock, tomato paste, thyme, and bay leaves and season with salt and pepper to taste. Bring to a boil, stirring continuously, then cover and simmer for 10 minutes.

Add the lima beans and dumplings to the pan, cover, and simmer for an additional 30 minutes.

Remove and discard the bay leaf before serving.

Spinach & Herb Frittata

serves 6-8

4 tablespoons olive oil

6 scallions, sliced

8 ounces frozen spinach, defrosted

6 large eggs

3 tablespoons finely chopped mixed fresh herbs

2 tablespoons freshly grated Parmesan cheese, plus extra for garnish

Pinch of salt

Freshly ground black pepper

Heat a nonstick skillet with a flameproof handle over medium heat. Add the oil and heat. Add the scallions and cook for about 2 minutes.

Add the spinach and cook until it just wilts.

Beat the eggs in a large bowl and season with salt and pepper to taste. Using a slotted spoon, transfer the spinach and scallions to the bowl of eggs and stir in the herbs. Pour the excess oil into a heatproof pitcher, then scrape off the crusty sediment from the bottom of the skillet.

Reheat the skillet. Add 2 tablespoons of the reserved oil. Pour in the egg mixture, smoothing it into an even layer. Cook, shaking the skillet occasionally, for 6 minutes or until the base is set when you lift up the side with a spatula.

Sprinkle the top of the frittata with the Parmesan cheese. Place the skillet under a preheated broiler and cook for 3 minutes or until the excess liquid is set and the cheese is golden.

Remove the skillet from the heat and slide the frittata onto a serving plate. Let stand for at least 5 minutes before cutting and garnishing with extra Parmesan cheese. Serve.

Ratatouille

serves 8

1 red bell pepper, seeded and quartered

1 orange bell pepper, seeded and quartered

1 green bell pepper, seeded and quartered

2 small eggplants, thickly sliced

2 tablespoons olive oil, plus extra for brushing

2 large onions, sliced

3 garlic cloves, finely chopped

3 medium zucchini, thickly sliced

5-6 medium tomatoes, peeled, seeded, and chopped

1½ teaspoons dried herbs

2 bay leaves

Salt and freshly ground pepper, to taste

Crusty bread, to serve

Preheat the broiler.

Put the bell pepper quarters, skin side up, on a baking sheet and broil until the skins are charred and blistered. Remove with tongs, put them into a plastic bag, tie the top, and let cool. Meanwhile, spread out the eggplant slices on the baking sheet, brush with oil, and broil for 5 minutes, until lightly browned. Turn, brush with oil, and broil for an additional 5 minutes, until lightly browned. Remove with tongs.

Remove the bell peppers from the bag and peel off the skins. Remove and discard the seeds and membranes and cut the flesh into strips. Dice the eggplant slices.

Heat the oil in a large pan or ovenproof casserole. Add the onions and cook over low heat, stirring occasionally, for 8–10 minutes, until lightly browned.

Add the garlic and zucchini, and cook, stirring occasionally, for an additional 10 minutes.

Stir in the bell peppers, eggplants, tomatoes, dried herbs, and bay leaves. Season to taste with salt and pepper, then cover and simmer over very low heat, stirring occasionally, for 25 minutes. Remove the lid and simmer, stirring occasionally, for an additional 25–35 minutes, until all the vegetables are tender.

Remove and discard the bay leaves. Serve the ratatouille immediately, if serving hot, or let cool, if serving at room temperature, accompanied by crusty bread.

Mushroom Stroganoff

serves 4

1 onion

2 tablespoons butter

1 pound mushrooms, diced

1 teaspoon tomato paste

1 teaspoon coarse-grain mustard

²/₃ cup sour cream

1 teaspoon paprika

Pinch of salt

Freshly ground black pepper

2 tablespoons chopped fresh parsley, for garnish

Finely chop the onion. Heat the butter in a large, heavy-bottom skillet. Add the onion and cook gently for 5–10 minutes, until soft. Meanwhile, trim and slice the mushrooms.

Add the mushrooms to the skillet and stir-fry for a few minutes until they start to soften. Stir in the tomato paste and mustard, then add the sour cream. Cook gently, stirring continuously, for 5 minutes.

Stir in the paprika and season with salt and pepper to taste. Garnish with the parsley and serve at once with long-grain rice or toast.

Italian Vegetable Stew

serves 4

1 red onion, sliced

2 leeks, sliced

4 garlic cloves, finely chopped

1 small squash, diced

1 eggplant, sliced

1 small celery root, diced

2 turnips, sliced

2 plum tomatoes, chopped

1 carrot, sliced

1 zucchini, sliced

2 red bell peppers, seeded and cut into strips

1 fennel bulb, sliced

6 ounces frozen spinach thawed and chopped

2 bay leaves

½ teaspoon fennel seeds

½ teaspoon chili powder

Pinch of dried thyme

Pinch of dried oregano

Pinch of sugar

½ cup extra virgin olive oil

1 cup vegetable stock

handful fresh basil leaves, torn

4 tablespoons chopped fresh flat-leaf parsley

Pinch of salt

Freshly ground black pepper

2 tablespoons freshly grated Parmesan cheese, for serving (optional)

Put the onion, leeks, garlic, squash, eggplant, celery root, turnips, tomatoes, carrot, zucchini, bell peppers, fennel, chard, bay leaves, fennel seeds, chili powder, thyme, oregano, sugar, olive oil, stock, and half the basil leaves into a large, heavy pan. Mix well and bring to a boil.

Reduce the heat, cover the pan, and simmer the vegetables for about 30 minutes, until tender.

Sprinkle in the remaining basil and the parsley and season with salt and pepper to taste.

Serve immediately, sprinkled with the cheese, if using.

Vegetable Lasagna

1 eggplant, peeled and sliced

3 tablespoons olive oil

2 garlic cloves, crushed

1 red onion, halved and sliced

3 mixed bell peppers, seeded and diced

1½ cups sliced mushrooms

2 celery ribs sliced

1 zucchini, peeled and diced

½ teaspoon chili powder

½ teaspoon ground cumin

2 tomatoes, chopped

One 14-5-ounce can chopped tomatoes, strained

2 tablespoons chopped fresh basil

8 no-precook lasagna verdi (green lasagna) sheets

Salt and freshly ground pepper, to taste

Cheese Sauce

2 tablespoons butter or margarine

1 tablespoon all-purpose flour

½ cup vegetable broth

1¼ cups milk

½ cup grated Cheddar cheese

1 teaspoon Dijon mustard

1 tablespoon chopped fresh basil

1 egg, beaten

Place the eggplant slices in a colander, sprinkle with salt, and let stand for 20 minutes. Rinse under cold water, drain, and reserve.

Preheat the oven to 350°F. Lightly grease a 9x13-inch baking pan.

Heat the oil in a saucepan. Add the garlic and onion and sauté for 1–2 minutes. Add the bell peppers, mushrooms, celery, and zucchini and cook, stirring constantly, for 3–4 minutes. Stir in the chili powder and cumin and cook for 1 minute. Mix in the tomatoes, strained canned tomatoes, and basil, and season to taste with salt and pepper.

To make the cheese sauce: Melt the butter in a saucepan. Stir in the flour and cook for 1 minute. Remove from the heat and gradually stir in the broth and milk. Return to the heat, then add half the cheese and the mustard. Simmer, stirring constantly, until thickened. Stir in the basil. Remove from the heat and stir in the egg.

Place half the lasagna sheets in the prepared baking pan. Top with half the vegetable mixture and half the eggplant slices. Repeat the layers, then spoon the cheese sauce on top. Sprinkle with the remaining cheese and bake in the preheated oven for 40 minutes, or until golden. Serve immediately.

Mexican Chili Corn Pie

serves 4

1 tablespoon corn oil

2 garlic cloves, crushed

1 red bell pepper, seeded and diced

1 green bell pepper, seeded and diced

1 celery stalk, diced

1 teaspoon hot chili powder

One 14.5-ounce can chopped tomatoes

2 cups corn

One 15-ounce can kidney beans, drained and rinsed

2 tablespoons chopped cilantro

Pinch of salt

Freshly ground black pepper

Topping

²/₃ cup cornmeal

1 tablespoon all-purpose flour

½ teaspoon salt

2 teaspoons baking powder

1 egg, beaten

6 tablespoons milk

1 tablespoon corn oil

1 cup grated cheddar cheese

Preheat the oven to 425°F.

Heat the oil in a large skillet and gently fry the garlic, bell peppers, and celery for 5–6 minutes until just softened.

Stir in the chili powder, tomatoes, corn, beans, and seasoning. Bring to a boil and simmer for 10 minutes. Stir in the cilantro and spoon into an ovenproof dish.

To make the topping, mix together the cornmeal, flour, salt, and baking powder. Make a well in the center, add the egg, milk, and oil and beat until a smooth batter is formed.

Spoon over the bell pepper and corn mixture and sprinkle with the cheese. Bake for 25–30 minutes until golden and firm. Serve immediately.

Spicy Fried Noodles

serves 4

1 pound medium egg noodles

4 ounces bean sprouts

2 tablespoons cut chives

3 tablespoons sunflower oil

1 garlic clove, crushed

4 fresh green chiles, seeded, sliced, and soaked in 2 tablespoons rice vinegar

Pinch of salt

Place the noodles in a bowl and cover with boiling water for 10 minutes. Drain and set aside.

Heat the oil in a preheated wok or large, heavy-bottom skillet. Add the crushed garlic and stir, then add the chiles and stir-fry for about 1 minute until fragrant.

Add the bean sprouts, stir, and then add the noodles. Stir in salt to taste and add the chives. Using 2 spoons or a wok scoop, lift and toss the noodles for 1 minute.

Transfer the noodles to a warmed serving dish, garnish with the reserved chives, and serve immediatley.

Cauliflower Bake

serves 4

1 small cauliflower, broken into florets

1 pound 5 ounces (about 4) potatoes, cut into cubes

10 cherry tomatoes

Sauce

2 tablespoons butter or margarine

1 leek, sliced

1 garlic clove, crushed

3 tablespoons all-purpose flour

1¼ cups whole milk

1 cup mixed grated cheeses, such as Cheddar, Parmesan, Gruyère, and Swiss cheese

½ teaspoon paprika

2 tablespoons chopped fresh Italian parsley

Salt and pepper to taste

Preheat the oven to 350°F.

Cook the cauliflower florets and potatoes in a saucepan of boiling water for 10 minutes. Drain and reserve until required.

To make the sauce, melt the butter in a large pan, add the sliced leek and garlic, and cook over low heat for 1 minute. Stir in the flour and cook, stirring constantly, for 1 minute, then remove the pan from the heat and gradually stir in the milk, ½ cup of the cheese, the paprika, and the chopped parsley. Return the pan to the heat and bring to a boil, stirring constantly. Season to taste with salt and pepper.

Transfer the cauliflower and potatoes to a deep, ovenproof dish and top with the cherry tomatoes. Pour the cheese sauce over to cover, and sprinkle with the remaining grated cheese.

Cook in the preheated oven for 20 minutes, or until the vegetables are cooked through and the cheese is golden brown and bubbling. Serve at once.

Mushroom & Bean Chili

4 tablespoons olive oil

1 cup mushrooms, chopped

1 large onion, chopped

1 garlic clove, chopped

1 green bell pepper, seeded and cut into strips

1 teaspoon paprika

1 teaspoon ground coriander

1 teaspoon ground cumin

½ teaspoon chili powder

One 14.5-ounce can of chopped tomatoes

⅔ cup vegetable stock

1 tablespoon tomato paste

One 14.5-ounce can red kidney beans, drained and rinsed

2 tablespoons chopped fresh cilantro

Pinch of salt

Freshly ground black pepper

Heat 1 tablespoon of the oil in a large skillet. Add the mushrooms and stir-fry until golden. Remove with a slotted spoon and set aside until required.

Add the remaining oil to the skillet. Add the onion, garlic, and bell pepper and cook for 5 minutes. Stir in the paprika, coriander, cumin, and chili powder and cook for an additional minute.

Add the tomatoes, stock, and tomato paste, stir well, then cover and cook for 20 minutes.

Add the reserved mushrooms and kidney beans and cook, covered, for an additional 20 minutes. Season with salt and pepper to taste and stir in the cilantro. Serve at once.

Vegetable Fritters

¾ cup whole wheat flour

Pinch of cayenne pepper

4 teaspoons olive oil

12 tablespoons cold water

1½ cups broccoli florets

1½ cups cauliflower florets

1 cup snow peas

1 large carrot, cut into sticks

1 red bell pepper, seeded and sliced

2 egg whites, beaten

oil, for deep-frying

pinch of salt

Sauce

⅔ cup pineapple juice

⅔ cup vegetable stock

2 tablespoons white wine vinegar

2 tablespoons brown sugar

2 teaspoons cornstarch

2 scallions, chopped

Sift the flour and a pinch of salt into a mixing bowl and add the cayenne pepper. Make a well in the center and gradually beat in the oil and cold water to make a smooth batter.

Bring a large pan of lightly salted water to a boil, cook the vegetables for 5 minutes, and drain well.

Whisk the egg whites until they form peaks and gently fold them into the flour batter.

Dip the vegetables into the batter, turning to coat well. Drain off any excess batter. Heat the oil in a deep-fat fryer to 350°F or until a cube of bread browns in 30 seconds. Fry the coated vegetables, in batches, for 1–2 minutes, until golden. Remove from the oil with a slotted spoon and drain on paper towels.

Place all of the sauce ingredients in a pan and bring to a boil, stirring, until the sauce is thickened and clear. Serve with the fritters.

Layered Vegetable Casserole

serves 4

1 tablespoon olive oil, for brushing

1 pound 8 ounces (about 5) white potatoes, peeled and thinly sliced

2 leeks, trimmed, thoroughly washed, and thinly sliced

2 beefsteak tomatoes, sliced

8 fresh basil leaves

1 garlic clove, finely chopped

Salt and freshly ground pepper, to taste

1¼ cups vegetable broth

Preheat the oven to 350°F.

Brush a Dutch oven or ovenproof casserole dish with a little of the olive oil. Prepare all the vegetables.

Place a layer of potato slices in the bottom of the dish, sprinkle with half of the basil leaves and cover with a layer of leeks. Top with a layer of tomato slices. Repeat these layers until all the vegetables are used up, ending with a layer of potatoes.

Stir the chopped garlic into the vegetable broth and season to taste with salt and pepper. Pour the broth over the vegetables and brush the top with the remaining olive oil.

Bake in the preheated oven for 1½ hours, or until the vegetables are tender and the topping is golden brown. Serve immediately.

Bean & Pasta Casserole

serves 4

1¼ cups dried cannellini beans, soaked overnight, and drained

8 ounces dried penne

6 tablespoons olive oil

Two 14.5-ounce cans vegetable broth

2 large onions, sliced

2 garlic cloves, chopped

2 bay leaves

1 teaspoon dried oregano

1 teaspoon dried thyme

5 tablespoons red wine

2 tablespoons tomato paste

2 celery ribs, sliced

1 fennel bulb, sliced

1½ cups sliced mushrooms

2 medium tomatoes, sliced

1 teaspoon brown sugar

½ cup dry white breadcrumbs

Salt and freshly ground pepper, to taste

Crusty bread, to serve

Preheat the oven to 350°F.

Put the beans in a large pan, add water to cover, and bring to a boil. Boil the beans rapidly for 20 minutes, then drain and set aside.

Cook the pasta in a large saucepan of boiling salted water, adding 1 tablespoon of the oil, for 3 minutes. Drain and set aside.

Put the beans in a large, ovenproof casserole dish, pour in the broth, and stir in the remaining oil, the onions, garlic, bay leaves, herbs, wine, and tomato paste. Bring to a boil, cover, and cook in the preheated oven for 2 hours.

Remove the casserole from the oven, add the reserved pasta, the celery, fennel, mushrooms, and tomatoes, and season to taste with salt and pepper. Stir in the sugar and sprinkle the breadcrumbs on top. Cover, return to the oven, and continue cooking for 1 hour. Serve immediately with warm crusty bread.

Four Cheese & Potato Layer Casserole

2 pounds potatoes, cut into wedges

2 tablespoons butter

1 red onion, halved and sliced

2 garlic cloves, crushed

¼ cup all-purpose flour

2½ cups whole milk

One 14.5-ounce can artichoke hearts in brine, drained and halved

⅓ cup frozen mixed vegetables, thawed

1 cup grated Swiss cheese

1 cupgrated cheddar cheese

½ cup crumbled Gorgonzola or any blue cheese

⅓ cup grated Parmesan cheese

1 cup bean curd, sliced

2 tablespoons chopped thyme

Pinch of salt

Freshly ground black pepper

Sprigs of fresh thyme, for garnish

Preheat the oven to 400°F.

Bring a pan of lightly salted water to a boil and cook the potato wedges for 10 minutes. Drain thoroughly.

Meanwhile, melt the butter in a pan. Add the sliced onion and garlic and fry over low heat, stirring frequently, for 2–3 minutes.

Stir the flour into the pan and cook for 1 minute. Gradually add the milk and bring to a boil, stirring continuously.

Reduce the heat and add the artichoke hearts, mixed vegetables, half of each of the 4 cheeses, and the bean curd to the pan, mixing well. Stir in the chopped thyme and season with salt and pepper to taste.

Arrange a layer of parboiled potato wedges in the base of a shallow ovenproof dish. Spoon the vegetable mixture over the top and cover with the remaining potato wedges. Sprinkle the rest of the 4 cheeses over the top.

Cook in the oven for 30 minutes or until the potatoes are cooked and the top is golden brown. Serve garnished with the sprigs of thyme

Winter Vegetable Stir-fry

serves 4

3 tablespoons
sesame oil

⅓ cup whole almonds

1 large carrot, cut into
thin strips

1 large turnip, cut into
thin strips

1 onion, sliced finely

1 garlic clove, crushed

3 celery stalks, sliced
finely

8 Brussels sprouts,
trimmed and halved

1½ cups cauliflower,
broken
into florets

1½ cups white cabbage,
shredded

2 teaspoons sesame
seeds

1 teaspoon grated fresh
gingerroot

½ teaspoon medium
chili powder

1 tablespoon chopped
fresh cilantro

1 tablespoon soy sauce

Pinch of salt

Freshly ground black
pepper

Heat the oil in a wok or large skillet. Stir-fry the almonds until lightly browned, then lift them out and drain on absorbent paper towels.

Add all the vegetables, except the cabbage, to the wok and stir-fry the vegetables briskly for 3–4 minutes.

Add the cabbage, sesame seeds, ginger, and chili powder and cook, stirring, for 2 minutes. Season to taste.

Add the chopped cilantro, soy sauce, and almonds, stirring gently to mix.

Serve the vegetables, garnished with the sprigs of cilantro.

Mushroom & Cauliflower Cheese Casserole

serves 4

1 medium head of cauliflower

4 tablespoons (½ stick) butter, plus 2 tablespoons for the topping

¾ cup mushrooms, sliced

Salt and freshly ground pepper, to taste

1 cup dry bread crumbs

2 tablespoons freshly grated Parmesan cheese

1 teaspoon dried oregano

1 teaspoon dried parsley

Preheat the oven to 450°F.

Break the cauliflower into small florets. Bring a large pan of salted water to a boil and cook the florets in the boiling water for 3 minutes. Remove from the heat, drain well, and transfer to a large shallow ovenproof or casserole dish.

Melt the 4 tablespoons of butter in a small skillet over medium heat. Add the mushrooms, stir to coat, and cook gently for 3 minutes. Remove from the heat and add to the cauliflower. Season to taste with salt and pepper.

Combine the bread crumbs, cheese, and herbs in a small mixing bowl, then sprinkle the mixture over the vegetables.

Dot the top of the casserole dish with 2 tablespoons of butter. Place the dish in the oven and bake for 15 minutes, or until the crumbs are golden brown and crisp. Serve warm.

Easy Spinach & Cheese Lasagna

serves 4

1 pound frozen spinach, thawed

Salt and pepper, to taste

1 pound ricotta cheese

8 sheets no-boil lasagna noodles

2½ cups strained tomatoes

1 cup mozzarella cheese, thinly sliced

1 tablespoon freshly grated Parmesan cheese

Preheat the oven to 350°F.

Put the spinach in a strainer and squeeze out any excess liquid. Put half of the spinach in the bottom of an 7x11-inch ovenproof baking dish and season to taste with salt and pepper.

Spread half the ricotta over the spinach, cover with half the lasagna sheets, then spoon over half the strained tomatoes. Arrange half the mozzarella cheese slices on top. Repeat the layers and top with a sprinkling of Parmesan cheese.

Bake in the preheated oven for 45–50 minutes, or until the top is golden and bubbling.

Vegetable Sesame Stir-fry

serves 4

2 tablespoons vegetable oil

3 garlic cloves, crushed

1 tablespoon sesame seeds, plus extra for garnish

2 celery stalks, sliced

2 baby corn cobs, sliced

1 cup white mushrooms, sliced

1 leek, sliced

1 zucchini, sliced

1 small red bell pepper, sliced

1 fresh green chile, sliced

½ cup cabbage, shredded

Rice or noodles, for serving

Sauce

½ teaspoon Chinese curry powder

2 tablespoons light soy sauce

1 tablespoon Chinese rice wine or dry sherry

1 teaspoon sesame oil

1 teaspoon cornstarch

4 tablespoons water

Heat the vegetable oil in a preheated wok or heavy skillet, swirling the oil around the bottom of the wok until it is almost smoking.

Reduce the heat slightly, add the garlic and sesame seeds, and cook for 30 seconds.

Add the celery, baby corn, mushrooms, leek, zucchini, bell pepper, chile, and cabbage and cook for 4–5 minutes, until the vegetables are beginning to soften.

To make the sauce: Mix together the curry powder, soy sauce, rice wine, sesame oil, cornstarch, and water.

Stir the sauce mixture into the wok until well combined with the other ingredients.

Bring to a boil and cook, stirring continuously, until the sauce thickens and clears.

Cook for 1 minute, then spoon into a warmed serving dish and garnish with sesame seeds.

Serve immediately, accompanied by the rice.

Winter Vegetable Stew

serves 4

1 onion, halved and sliced

3 garlic cloves, crushed

8 ounces frozen spinach thawed

1 fennel bulb, cut into eighths

1 red bell pepper, seeded and cubed

1 tablespoon all-purpose flour

1¾ cups vegetable stock

6 tablespoons dry white wine

One 10.5-ounce can chickpeas, drained

1 bay leaf

1 teaspoon ground coriander

½ teaspoon paprika

Pinch of salt

Freshly ground black pepper

Heat the olive oil in a dutch oven. Add about 4 tablespoons water the onion and garlic and sauté over low heat, stirring frequently, for 1 minute. Add the spinach and cook, stirring occasionally, for 4 minutes.

Add the fennel pieces and the bell pepper and cook, stirring continuously, for 2 minutes.

Stir in the flour and cook, stirring continuously, for 1 minute.

Add the stock, wine, chickpeas, bay leaf, coriander, and paprika, cover, and simmer for 30 minutes.

Season with salt and pepper to taste and serve immediately straight from the casserole.

Pasta & Bean Casserole

serves 6

8 ounces dried navy beans, soaked overnight and drained

6 tablespoons olive oil

2 large onions, sliced

2 garlic cloves, chopped

2 bay leaves

1 teaspoon dried oregano

1 teaspoon dried thyme

5 tablespoons red wine

2 tablespoons tomato paste

3½ cups vegetable broth

8 ounces dried penne, or other short pasta shapes

2 celery ribs, sliced

1 fennel bulb, sliced

1 cup sliced mushrooms

6 medium tomatoes, sliced

Salt and freshly ground pepper, to taste

1 teaspoon firmly packed light brown sugar

1 cup dry white bread crumbs

Salad greens and crusty bread, to serve

Preheat oven to 350°F.

Place the beans in a pan, cover with water, and bring to a boil. Boil rapidly for 20 minutes, then drain.

Place the beans in a large Dutch oven or ovenproof casserole dish, stir in 5 tablespoons of the olive oil, the onions, garlic, bay leaves, herbs, wine, and tomato paste, and pour in the vegetable broth. Bring to a boil, then cover the casserole, and place it in the preheated oven, and bake for 2 hours.

Towards the end of the cooking time, bring a large pan of salted water to the boil, add the pasta and the remaining olive oil and cook for 3 minutes. Drain and set aside.

Remove the casserole dish from the oven and add the pasta, celery, fennel, mushrooms, and tomatoes, and season to taste with salt and pepper. Stir in the sugar, and sprinkle the bread crumbs over the stew. Cover the casserole, return it to the oven, and continue cooking for 1 hour.

Serve hot with salad greens and crusty bread.

Penne & Eggplants Stuffed with Cheese

serves 4

8 ounces dried penne or other short pasta shapes

4 tablespoons olive oil, plus extra for brushing

2 eggplants

1 large onion, chopped

2 garlic cloves, crushed

One 14.5-ounce can chopped tomatoes

2 teaspoons dried oregano

⅓ cup mozzarella cheese, thinly sliced

⅓ cup freshly grated Parmesan cheese

5 tablespoons dry breadcrumbs

Salt and freshly ground pepper, to taste

Fresh salad greens, for serving

Preheat oven to 400°F. Brush a baking sheet with oil.

Bring a large pan of lightly salted water to a boil. Add the pasta and 1 tablespoon of the olive oil, bring back to a boil, and cook for 8–10 minutes or until the pasta is just tender, but still firm to the bite. Drain, return to the pan, cover, and keep warm.

Cut the eggplants in half lengthwise and score around the inside with a sharp knife, being careful not to pierce the shells. Scoop out the flesh with a spoon. Brush the insides of the shells with olive oil. Chop the flesh and set aside.

Heat the remaining oil in a skillet. Sauté the onion over low heat for 5 minutes, until softened. Add the garlic and fry for 1 minute. Add the chopped eggplant and cook, stirring frequently, for 5 minutes. Add the tomatoes and oregano and season with salt and pepper to taste. Bring to a boil and simmer for 10 minutes until thickened. Remove the skillet from the heat and stir in the pasta.

Arrange the eggplant shells in a single layer on the oiled baking sheet. Divide half of the tomato-and-pasta mixture among them. Sprinkle the slices of mozzarella over, then pile the remaining tomato and pasta mixture on top. Mix the Parmesan cheese and breadcrumbs together and sprinkle over the top, patting it lightly into the mixture.

Bake in the preheated oven for approximately 25 minutes or until the topping is golden brown and bubbly. Serve hot with a selection of mixed fresh salad greens.

Spicy Chickpea Casserole

1 tablespoon cumin seeds

2 tablespoons coriander seeds

2 teaspoons dried oregano or thyme

5 tablespoons vegetable oil

2 onions, chopped

1 red bell pepper, seeded and cut into ¾-inch chunks

1 eggplant, peeled and cut into ¾-inch chunks

2 garlic cloves, chopped

1 fresh green chile, chopped

One 14.5-ounce can chopped tomatoes

One 10.5 ounce can chickpeas, drained and rinsed

16 green beans, cut into ¾-inch lengths

2½ cups vegetable stock

3 tablespoons chopped fresh cilantro, plus extra leaves to garnish

Dry-roast the seeds in a heavy-bottom skillet for a few seconds, until aromatic. Add the oregano and cook for an additional few seconds. Remove from the heat, transfer to a mortar, and crush with a pestle.

Heat the oil in a large, ovenproof casserole dish. Cook the onions, bell pepper, and eggplant for 10 minutes, until softened. Add the ground seed mixture, garlic, and chile, and cook for an additional 2 minutes.

Add the tomatoes, chickpeas, green beans, and stock. Bring to a boil, cover, and simmer gently for 1 hour, then stir in the chopped cilantro.

Serve immediately, garnished with fresh cilantro leaves.

Potato & Mushroom Casserole

serves 4

2 tablespoons butter

1 pound waxy potatoes, thinly sliced and parboiled

2 cups sliced mixed mushrooms

1 tablespoon chopped rosemary

4 tablespoons snipped chives, plus extra to garnish

2 garlic cloves, crushed

²/₃ cup heavy cream

Salt and pepper

Grease a shallow round ovenproof or casserole dish with butter.

Layer a quarter of the potatoes in the bottom of the dish. Arrange a quarter of the mushrooms on top of the potatoes and sprinkle with a quarter of the rosemary, chives, and garlic. Continue making layers in the same order, finishing with a layer of potatoes on top.

Pour the heavy cream over the top of the potatoes. Season to taste with salt and pepper.

Cook in a preheated oven, 375°F, for about 45 minutes or until the pie is golden brown on top and piping hot.

Garnish with snipped chives and serve at once straight from the dish.

Vegetable Casserole with Potatoes & Cheese

1 carrot, diced

2 cups cauliflower florets

(2 cups broccoli florets

1 fennel bulb, sliced

12 green beans, halved

2 tablespoons butter

2½ tablespoons all-purpose flour

⅔ cup vegetable stock

⅔ cup dry white wine

⅔ cup whole milk

1½ cups cremini mushrooms, cut into fourths

2 tablespoons chopped fresh sage

Topping

2 pounds (about 6) starchy potatoes, peeled and diced

2 tablespoons butter

4 tablespoons plain yogurt

1 cup freshly grated Parmesan cheese

1 teaspoon fennel seeds

Salt and pepper, to taste

Preheat the oven to 375°F.

Cook the carrot, cauliflower, broccoli, fennel, and beans in a pan of boiling water for 10 minutes, until just tender. Drain the vegetables and reserve.

Melt the butter in a pan. Stir in the flour and cook over low heat for 1 minute. Remove from the heat and stir in the stock, wine, and milk. Return to the heat and bring the mixture to a boil, stirring constantly, until thickened. Stir in the reserved vegetables, the mushrooms, and the chopped sage.

To make the topping, cook the potatoes in a pan of boiling water for 10–15 minutes. Drain and mash with the butter, yogurt, and half the cheese. Stir in the fennel seeds. Season to taste with salt and pepper.

Spoon the vegetable mixture into a deep-dish pie or tart pan. Spoon the potato mixture over the top, sprinkle the remaining Parmesan cheese over the potatoes, and bake for 30–35 minutes, or until golden. Serve immediately.

Tuscan Bean Stew

serves 4

1 large fennel bulb

2 tablespoons olive oil

1 red onion, cut into small wedges

2–4 garlic cloves, sliced

One 8-ounce eggplant, peeled and cut into chunks

2 tablespoons tomato paste

2–2½ cups vegetable broth

3 ripe tomatoes, chopped

A few sprigs of fresh oregano

One 14.5-ounce can cranberry beans

One 14.5-ounce can cannellini beans

1 yellow bell pepper, seeded and cut into small strips

1 zucchini, sliced into semicircles

⅓ cup pitted black olives

1 ounce Parmesan cheese, freshly shaved

Salt and freshly ground pepper, to taste

Crusty bread, to serve

Trim the fennel and reserve any feathery fronds, then cut the bulb into thin strips. Heat the oil in a large, heavy-bottom pan with a tight fitting lid, and cook the onion, garlic, and fennel strips, stirring frequently, for 5–8 minutes, or until softened.

Add the eggplant and cook, stirring frequently, for 5 minutes. Blend the tomato paste with a little of the broth in a pitcher and pour over the fennel mixture, then add the remaining broth, and the tomatoes, and oregano. Bring to boil, then reduce the heat and simmer, covered, for 15 minutes, or until the tomatoes have begun to collapse.

Drain and rinse the beans, then drain again. Add them to the pan with the yellow bell pepper, zucchini, and olives. Simmer for an additional 15 minutes, or until the vegetables are tender. Taste and adjust the seasoning.

Place in bowls, and garnish with the Parmesan shavings and the reserved fennel fronds, accompanied by crusty bread.

Chili Bean Stew

2 tablespoons olive oil

1 onion, chopped

2–4 garlic cloves, chopped

2 fresh red chiles, seeded and sliced

One 15-ounce can kidney beans, drained and rinsed

One 14.5-ounce can cannellini beans, drained and rinsed

One 10.5-ounce can chickpeas, drained and rinsed

1 tablespoon tomato paste

3¾ cups chicken broth

1 red bell pepper, seeded and chopped

4 tomatoes, coarsely chopped

1½ cups fava beans, fresh (shelled) or frozen

1 tablespoon chopped fresh cilantro

Freshly ground pepper, to taste

Sour cream, to serve

Chopped cilantro and paprika, to garnish

Heat the oil in a large, heavy-bottom pan with a tight-fitting lid, and cook the onion, garlic, and chiles, stirring frequently, for 5 minutes, or until softened. Add the kidney beans, cannellini beans, and chickpeas. Blend the tomato paste with a little of the broth in a pitcher and pour over the bean mixture, then add the remaining broth. Bring to a boil, then reduce the heat and simmer for 10–15 minutes.

Add the red bell pepper, tomatoes, fava beans, and pepper to taste and simmer for 15–20 minutes, or until all the vegetables are tender. Stir in the chopped cilantro.

Serve the stew topped with spoonfuls of sour cream and garnished with chopped cilantro and a pinch of paprika.

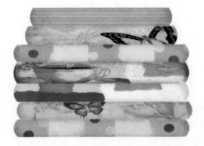

Chunky Vegetable Soup

2 carrots, sliced

1 onion, diced

1 garlic clove, crushed

4-6 small new potatoes, diced

2 celery ribs, sliced

1 cup button mushrooms, quartered

One 14.5-ounce can chopped tomatoes, with their juice

2½ cups vegetable broth

1 bay leaf

1 teaspoon dried mixed herbs or 1 tablespoon chopped fresh mixed herbs

½ cup corn kernels, frozen or canned, drained

1 cup shredded green cabbage

Freshly ground pepper, to taste

Crusty whole wheat or white bread, to serve

Put the carrots, onion, garlic, potatoes, celery, mushrooms, tomatoes, and broth into a large pan. Stir in the bay leaf and herbs. Bring to a boil, then reduce the heat, cover, and let simmer for 25 minutes.

Add the corn and cabbage and return to a boil. Reduce the heat, cover, and let simmer for 5 minutes, or until the vegetables are tender.

Remove and discard the bay leaf and season to taste with pepper.

Ladle into warmed bowls and serve at once with crusty bread.

Lentil & Rice Stew

serves 4

1 cup red lentils

¼ cup long-grain rice

5 cups vegetable broth

1 leek, trimmed, thoroughly washed, and cut into chunks

3 garlic cloves, crushed

One 14.5-ounce can chopped tomatoes

1 teaspoon ground cumin

1 teaspoon chili powder

1 teaspoon garam masala

1 red bell pepper, seeded and sliced

1 cup small broccoli florets

8 baby corn, halved lengthwise

1 cup green beans, halved

1 tablespoon shredded fresh basil

Salt and freshly ground pepper, to taste

Fresh basil sprigs, to garnish

Place the lentils, rice, and vegetable broth in a dutch oven and cook over low heat, stirring occasionally, for 20 minutes.

Add the leek, garlic, tomatoes and their juice, ground cumin, chili powder, garam masala, sliced bell pepper, broccoli, baby corn, and green beans to the casserole.

Bring the mixture to a boil, reduce the heat, cover, and simmer for an additional 10–15 minutes, or until all the vegetables are tender.

Add the shredded basil and season with salt and pepper to taste.

Garnish with fresh basil sprigs and serve immediately.

Spicy Vegetable Cobbler

serves 4

1 large onion, sliced

2 zucchini, sliced

1 cup sliced mushrooms

2 large carrots, coarsely chopped

One 10.5-ounce can black-eyed peas, drained and rinsed

One 14.5-ounce can cannellini beans, drained and rinsed

One 14.5-ounce can chopped tomatoes

1 teaspoon mild chili powder

Salt and freshly ground pepper, to taste

Topping

1¼ cups all-purpose flour, plus extra for dusting

2 teaspoons baking powder

½ teaspoons paprika

Pinch of salt

3 tablespoons butter

4 tablespoons milk

Preheat the oven to 400°F.

Put the onion, zucchini, mushrooms, carrots, black-eyed peas, cannellini beans, and tomatoes with their juices in an ovenproof casserole. Sprinkle the chili powder over the vegetables, and season to taste with salt and pepper. Transfer to the preheated oven and bake for 15 minutes.

Meanwhile, to make the cobbler topping, sift the flour, baking powder, paprika, and salt into a large mixing bowl. Rub in the butter until the mixture resembles fine breadcrumbs, then stir in enough of the milk to make a smooth dough. Transfer to a lightly floured board, knead lightly, then roll out to a thickness of about ½ inch. Cut out circles using a 2-inch cookie cutter.

Remove the casserole from the oven, arrange the dough circles over the top, then return to the oven and bake for 30 minutes, or until the cobbler topping has risen and is lightly golden. Serve immediately.

Chinese Vegetable Stir Fry

4 tablespoons vegetable oil

2 carrots, sliced

1 zucchini, sliced

4 baby corn cobs, halved lengthwise

1½ cup cauliflower florets

1 leek, sliced

½ cup water chestnuts, halved

1 cup (2 sticks) firm bean curd, cubed

1¼ cups vegetable stock

1 teaspoon salt

2 teaspoons dark brown sugar

2 teaspoons dark soy sauce

2 tablespoons dry sherry

1 tablespoon cornstarch

2 tablespoons water

1 tablespoon chopped fresh

Cilantro, for garnish

Heat the oil in a preheated wok until it is almost smoking. Reduce the heat slightly, add the carrots, zucchini, baby corn, cauliflower, and leek and cook for 2–3 minutes.

Stir in the water chestnuts, bean curd, stock, salt, sugar, soy sauce, and sherry and bring to a boil. Reduce the heat, cover, and simmer for 20 minutes.

Blend the cornstarch with the water to form a smooth paste.

Stir the cornstarch mixture into the wok. Bring the sauce to a boil and cook, stirring continuously, until it thickens and clears.

Transfer the stir fry to a warmed serving dish, sprinkle with the cilantro, and serve immediately.

Risotto with Spring Vegetables

serves 4

5 cups vegetable stock

Large pinch of saffron threads

4 tablespoons butter

1 tablespoon olive oil

1 onion, chopped

2 garlic cloves, finely chopped

1 cup risotto rice

3 tablespoons dry white wine

1 bay leaf

2 cups mixed spring vegetables, such as asparagus spears, green beans, baby carrots, baby fava beans, and young green peas, thawed if frozen

2 tablespoons chopped fresh flat-leaf parsley

1 cup grated Parmesan cheese

Salt and pepper

Put a generous ⅓ cup of the stock into a small bowl, crumble in the saffron threads, and let steep. Reserve ⅔ cup of the remaining stock and heat the remainder in a pan.

Melt 2 tablespoons of the butter with the oil in a separate large pan. Add the onion and garlic and cook over low heat, stirring occasionally, for 5 minutes, until softened. Stir in the rice and cook, stirring constantly, for 1–2 minutes, until all the grains are coated and glistening.

Pour in the wine and cook, stirring constantly, for a few minutes, until all the alcohol has evaporated. Season to taste with salt and pepper. Pour in the hot stock and the saffron mixture, add the bay leaf, and bring to a boil, stirring constantly.

Reduce heat to low, adding a lid to the pan and cook for 20 minutes. If using fresh vegetables, slice the asparagus spears, green beans, and carrots and blanch all the vegetables in boiling water for 5 minutes. Drain and reserve.

Stir the reserved stock into the rice mixture, if it seems dry, and add the mixed vegetables, sprinkling them evenly over the top. Re-cover and cook on low for an additional 10 minutes, until the vegetables are cooked.

Remove and discard the bay leaf. Gently stir in the parsley, the remaining butter, and the Parmesan and serve immediately.

Index

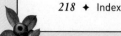